Quirky Critter Devotions

Tyndale House Publishers
Carol Stream, Illinois

52 Wild Wonders for Kids

QUIRKY CRITTER DEVOTIONS

ANNETTE WHIPPLE

bare-hearted glass frog © Allen Lara Gonzalez; dusty glass frog © petrdd; tadpole icon © parkjisun; crayfish icon © 4urbrand; fish eggs icon © Prashanth Rapolu; female American bullfrog and eastern painted turtle © David Byron Keener; spring peeper peeping © Paul Tessier; American bullfrog farm © wasin suriyawan; tree frog, tadpoles, king cobra closeup, and chameleon © Kurit afshen; bullfrog in water © Karl-Heinz Müller/Unsplash; ruby-throated hummingbird and loon close-up © Jeremy Hynes/Unsplash; hummingbird © Holly Miller-Pollack; hummingbird at feeder © Joshua J. Cotten/Unsplash; flies icon © Marie Van den Broeck; mosquito icon © Alisa Anderson; fly icon © Eric Miller; kiwi bird © Vee Snijders; eel icon © ABDUL LATIF; north island brown kiwi © Lakeview Images; green grapes © SHTRAUS DMYTRO; dried raisins © akepong srichaichana; almonds © suriya yapin; ripe kiwi © Atlas Studio; leech icon © Andy Mc; loon taking off © Brett Swain; baby loon © Agnieszka Bacal; hoatzin © Jose Rui Santos; hoatzin close-up © Patrik Hansson; hoatzins perched on branch © Morten Ross; turkey vulture © Dev Leigh/ Unsplash; poop icon © Doodle Icons; animal skeleton icon © Laymik; turkey vulture in flight © Pascal De Munck; flock circling © Ezume Images; starling © Daniil Komov/Unsplash; berry icon © DinosoftLab; seed icon © Fahmi Somdi Std; starling in flight © photomaster; starlings on branches © Menno Schaefer; murmuration © Philip Reeve; murmuration at beach © Jon Ingall; large flock of starlings and two owlets © Albert Beukhof; burrowing owl © Meg Jerrard/Unsplash; owl close-up © Steve Harvey/Unsplash; owl pair © Dennis Von Linden; owl flying © Chase D'animulls; owl guarding nest © Voodison328; stonefish © David Clode/Unsplash; reef stonefish © Vladimir Wrangel; pink stonefish © Kristina Vackova; whale shark from below © Ishan @seefromthesky/Unsplash; plankton icon © Uswa KDT; whale shark © Krzysztof Odziomek; whale shark feeding © Fata Morgana by Andrew Marriott; whale shark underwater © Lindsey Lu; fathead minnow breeding male © Rankin1958/Wikimedia; fathead minnows © Robert Aguilar, Smithsonian Environmental Research Center; algae icon © Anggun; fathead minnow in green water photo courtesy of the Missouri Department of Conservation; pacific seahorse © David A Litman; giant seahorses © SunflowerMomma; 'O'opu nopili © Hawaii Biological Survey, Bishop Museum; Sicyopterus stimpsoni by USFWS, public domain; blobfish © by Robert Zugaro/Museums Victoria; Mr. Blobby by Kerryn Parkinson, Australian Museum © NORFANZ Founding Parties; psychrolutes marcidus © by Amanda Hay/ Australian Museum; shell icon © Dmitry Vasiliev; iguana © Meg Jerrard/Unsplash; mockingbird © Mark Olsen/Unsplash; Galapagos iguana © Maridav; marine iguana © Natursports; iguana with blue-footed birds © reisegraf.ch; seaweed icon © Julia Kitaeva; eastern garter snake © Bill Keim/iNaturalist/Wikimedia; common garter snake © Brian Gratwicke/Wikimedia; garter snake on dead leaves © Jeff Holcombe; garter snake defensive position © Jason Patrick Ross; group of red-sided garter snake © Jukka Palm; common garter snake tongue © Ron Rowan Photography; short-horned lizard © J. Dullum/USFWS; giant horned lizard © Petlin Dmitry; American crocodile © SolieT; turtle icon © BGBOXXX Design; crocodile underwater © Jesus Cobaleda; crocodile hatching © hxdbzxy; open-mouthed crocodile and black widow spiders with egg sac © Mark Kostich; baby crocodiles © dioch; crocodiles by a river © Ondrej Prosicky; midland painted turtle © Brian Lasenby; painted turtle © Gerald A. DeBoer; western painted turtle © Dennis Diehl; turtle hiding © WilleeCole Photography; king cobra © GoodFocused; Ophiophagus Hannah © Andreas Rose; king cobra eating © Mufti Adi Utomo; king cobra nest © Jim Lambert; panther chameleon closeup © Bildagentur Zoonar GmbH; chameleon tail © Jan Bures; peacock spider © Jürgen Otto/Wikimedia; Maratus hortorum and jumping spider © Jean and Fred Hort/Flickr; common peacock spider © Shane Walker/iNaturalist; Maratus Pavonis © bronwynking/Wikimedia; flea icon © Pham Duy Phuong Hung; argyroteta aquatica © Norbert Schuller Baupi/Wikimedia; underwater spider © D. Kucharski K. Kucharska; diving bell spider © Stefan K., Hetz, Berlin, Germany; house spider with prey © Ethan Quin; female house spider © Eric Crudup; house spider with catch © Aleksandar Dickov; Achaearanea tepidariorum © Mad Max/Wikimedia; orange longlegged spider © Olivier Laurent Photos; pholcus phalangioide © Tomasz Klejdysz; daddy longlegs closeups © Olei/Wikimedia; wolf spider on egg sac © MMCez; female wolf spider with babies © Philip Steury Photography; brown widow spider © phonecat; female redback spider © iSKYDANCER; closeup black widow © Malpolon; larva icon © Anton Gajdosik; jumping spider © Joyce LCY; Bagheera kiplingi © Sundar perumal; bagheera kiplingi on leaf © Wirestock Creators; lizard panther chameleon © PetlinDmitry; blue tang fish © bluehand; burrowing owls © David McGowen/Adobe Stock; bee queens © Kuttelvaserova Stuchelova; turkey vulture open wings © Christian Musat; sea urchin © Zoltan Major; wolf spider close-up © Rob Hainer; blue tang © Tatiana Gordievskaia; reef fish © pkproject; hippo fish © bekirevren; blue surgeon fish © Katjabakurova.

Visit Tyndale online at tyndale.com.

Visit Tyndale's website for kids at tyndale.com/kids.

Visit the author online at annettewhipple.com.

Quirky Critter Devotions: 52 Wild Wonders for Kids

Designed by Sarah Susan Richardson

Edited by Deborah King

For manufacturing information regarding this product, please call 1-855-277-9400.

For information about special discounts for bulk purchases, please contact Tyndale House Publishers at csresponse@tyndale.com, or call 1-855-277-9400.

Library of Congress Cataloging-in-Publication Data

A catalog record for this book is available from the Library of Congress.

ISBN 978-1-4964-7700-2

Printed in China

30 29 28 27 26 25 24
7 6 5 4 3 2 1

For my friends and family
who help me live in wonder.

Contents

Mammals

Insects

Amphibians

Birds

Fish

Reptiles

Spiders

About **6,500** species of mammals live around the world, both on land and in oceans. Hair or fur covers mammals' bodies. Almost all give birth to live young (rather than laying eggs like birds, reptiles, and some other creatures), and they produce nutrient-rich milk to feed their babies.

As warm-blooded animals, mammals keep a constant body temperature even when the weather changes. Some migrate or hibernate with the change of seasons.

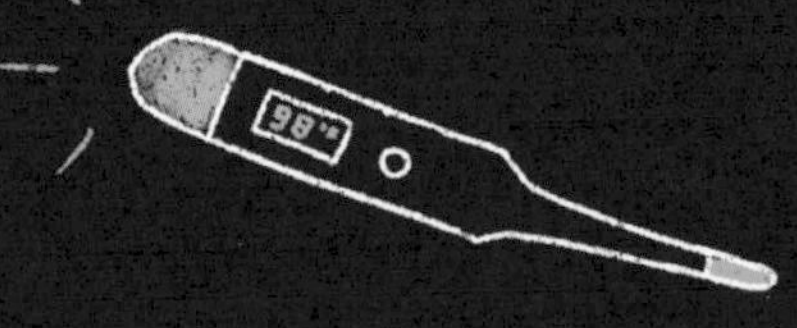

MAMMALS

Gray Wolf

Scientific Name: *Canis lupus*

Awhooooooo!

Gray wolves live in groups called packs in parts of North America, Europe, and Asia. The size of packs varies, but 5 to 9 wolves is common. A male and female pair form a pack with their offspring.

During spring and summer, as wolf pups grow, they stay in their den for the first 8 to 10 weeks of life. At first the mother cares for all the needs of her litter of pups. After a couple of weeks, the pups begin to see and hear, and they start to move around. Soon the pack works like a family, and they all help tend to the pups' needs. The pups begin to leave the den and learn how to hunt by playing. Young wolves hunt with the pack when they're about 6 to 8 months old.

Once fall arrives, the wolf pack becomes nomadic, meaning they move from place to place. A pack of gray wolves usually moves at night, covering long distances—up to 125 miles (200 kilometers) at a time. Typically, they travel about as fast as humans walk at a brisk pace, but they are capable of great speed. Gray wolves run as fast as 40 miles per hour (64 kilometers per hour).

Known for their hunting skills, gray wolves use scent to find their prey. In packs, they often take down large animals like moose, elk, musk oxen, and reindeer—targeting the weak, old, or immature. Lone wolves hunt small prey like beavers and rabbits.

Gray wolves use vocalizations like howling to find each other. You may not talk with howls, but every message you type and every word you say communicates with others. Do you send kind and loving messages to friends, family, and strangers? Use your words to glorify God by being a friend and encourager to all.

Make a list of several friends or family members you want to encourage this week.

Encourage one another and build one another up, just as you are doing.

1 THESSALONIANS 5:11

Father, help me to be an encouragement in my words and messages to people I know. In Jesus' name, amen.

Wild Wonder

Gray wolves can eat 20 pounds (9 kilograms) of meat at once.

Creature Connection

Follow the steps below to make an origami wolf. You'll need a few sheets of thin, square paper to get started. Write encouraging notes to 2 or 3 friends on the pieces of paper and fold each one into the shape of a wolf. Leave them in places where your friends will find them.

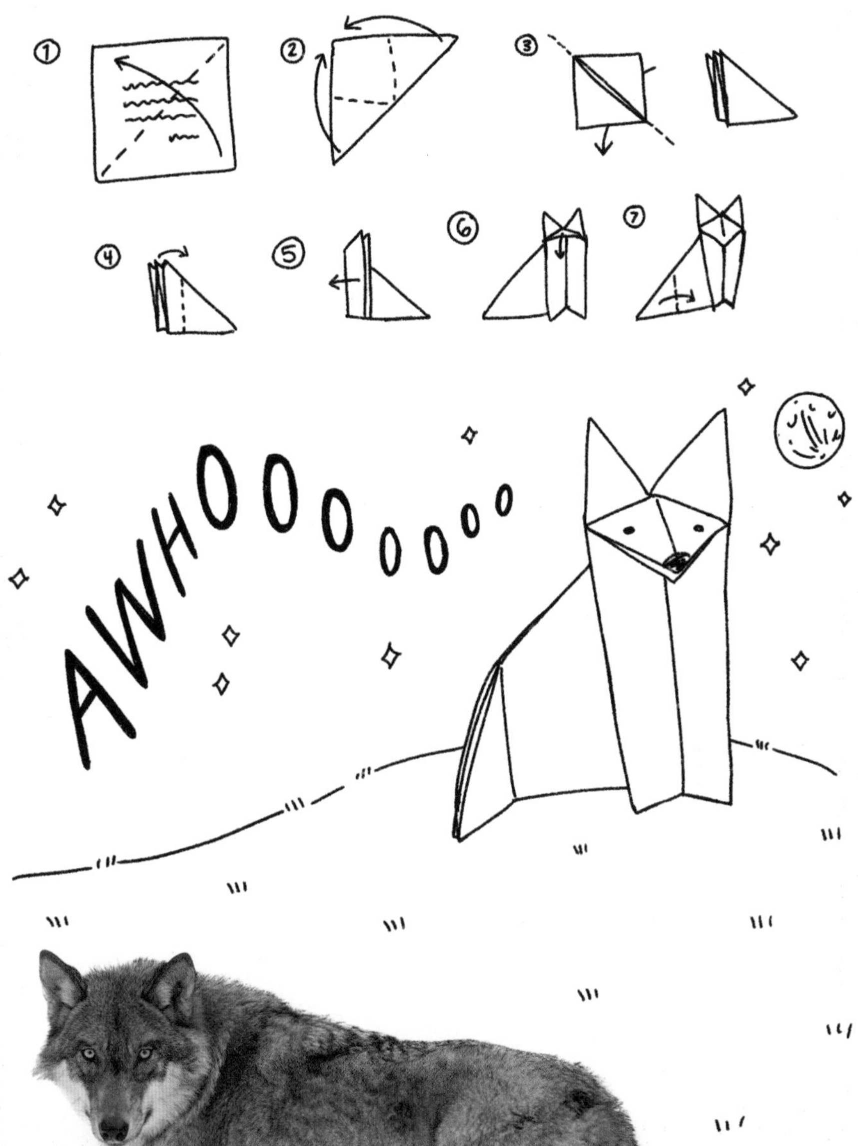

Pangolin

Scientific Names: *Manis crassicaudata*, *Manis culionensis*, *Manis javanica*, and more

Mash-Up

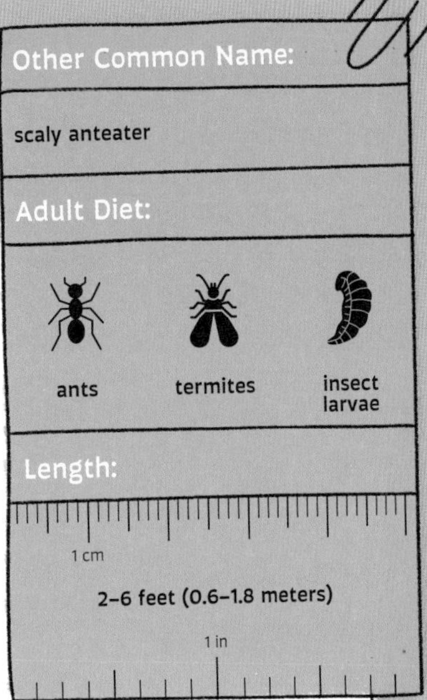

Other Common Name:
scaly anteater
Adult Diet:
ants
termites
insect larvae
Length:
1 cm
2–6 feet (0.6–1.8 meters)
1 in

With huge claws, the pangolin digs into termite mounds and ant nests as it sniffs for its next meal. It easily snatches small insects with its 2-foot-long (61-centimeter) sticky tongue. But it doesn't eat much—only about 45 grams of food a day. That's the same weight as 4 tablespoons of rice.

Today, pangolins live only on the continents of Asia and Africa in tropical forests, woodlands, and savannas. Some dig their own burrows. Other pangolins shelter in caves, hollow trees, abandoned homes, or between rocks.

When they feel threatened, pangolins spray a nasty-smelling liquid. They also roll tightly into a ball to protect their hairy stomach while their outer scales stop predators like leopards and lions. These mammals are born with scales covering their bodies. The sharp scales overlap like body armor.

Pangolins' scales protect them against most natural predators but not against humans. They are sold illegally and considered the most highly trafficked animal in the world. They are killed for their scales and meat. All 8 species of pangolins are endangered or threatened with extinction today.

Pangolins seem like a mash-up of reptiles (scales), wombats (digging claws), amphibians (sticky tongue), and skunks (stinky spray). Yet they are their own unique design. You are unique too—God's design. He made you to look a little bit like your mom and a little bit like your dad—and he also made you exactly who he wanted you to be. Look in the mirror today and thank God for how he created you.

Write down the physical characteristics you like best about yourself. Think about your friends and family. Which characteristics do you share with loved ones?

I praise you, for I am fearfully and wonderfully made.

PSALM 139:14

Dear God, thank you for carefully making me just the way you planned. In Jesus' name, amen.

Wild Wonder

The pangolin doesn't have teeth, so its stomach "chews" the bugs it eats.

Creature Connection

Draw a picture of yourself and label all of your unique physical characteristics. Notice the little things like your freckles, multiple colors in your eyes, and the unique shade of your skin in addition to features like your height and hair color.

Pygmy Marmoset

Scientific Names: *Callithrix pygmaea*, *Cebuella pygmaea*, and *Cebuella niveiventris*

The Smallest Monkey

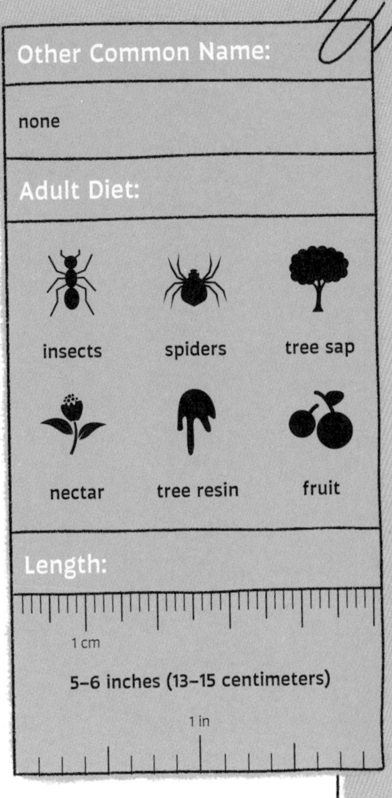

The pygmy marmoset is about as tall as your hand, with a tail longer than its body. This smallest monkey in the world can leap as far as 15 feet (5 meters) from tree to tree.

Pygmy marmosets live in small groups along the river floodplains of South America. A baby nurses for 3 months, feeding on its mother's milk, and the father and other group members care for it too. They all take turns grooming and carrying the baby monkey. Their group is like a family.

After sleeping in a roost at night, a pygmy marmoset group leaves at sunrise. They feed for 30 to 90 minutes on the sticky gum a tree secretes during the night. Then it's time to play, groom, and hang out together. In the middle of the day, the group rests. Later they eat more and then return to their roost.

Pygmy marmosets may not watch clocks, but they follow a daily schedule. Think about your daily routine. Do you relax and play? Work and learn? What time of day do you read the Bible and talk to God? Make time to spend with God, especially when you're busy.

Monkeys and Apes: What's the Difference?

	Monkeys	Apes
Kinds	hundreds of species	chimpanzee, bonobo, gibbon, gorilla, orangutan
Tail	almost all have tails	no tails
Intelligence	intelligent	very intelligent
Language	sounds, gestures	sounds, gestures, sign language
Movement	most run on branches, some swing through trees	swing through trees
Size	smaller, narrow chested	larger, broad chested

List some things you would like to do today (or tomorrow). Then number each one in order of importance.

O God, you are my God; earnestly I seek you.

PSALM 63:1

Heavenly Father, thank you for giving me 24 hours each day. Help me to prioritize spending time with you daily. In Jesus' name, amen.

Wild Wonder

At birth, pygmy marmosets weigh about half an ounce (15 grams), or about as much as a tablespoon of water.

Creature Connection

Write down all the things you need to do in a day. Include commitments like school, appointments, extracurricular activities, and meals. Then add other things you want to do, like watching television, making a craft, playing a video game, or exploring a creek. If you're busy, it's worth it to skip part of one activity to make time for God.

MY SCHEDULE

Little Brown Bat

Scientific Name: *Myotis lucifugus*

Winter Choices

Other Common Name:

none

Adult Diet:

moths beetles mayflies

Length:

1 cm

2.5–4 inches (6–10 centimeters)

1 in

Throughout much of the United States and Canada, colonies of little brown bats spend their days hiding. They hang upside down in nesting sites called roosts, which can be inside buildings, under rocks, or in piles of wood. Colonies can contain hundreds or thousands of little brown bats.

They may be little, but these bats are huge eaters. Little brown bats hunt a few hours after sunset. They eat about half their weight in bugs each night when not hibernating. A new mother eats even more.

Some people think bats are blind because their eyes are small. Bats can see, but in the dark they don't rely on their vision. Instead, they use their supersense of echolocation to find food and objects. Echolocation uses a really high sound frequency that humans cannot hear. The bats call about 20 times each second. The sound bounces off an object and returns to the bat like an echo. This is how they are master insect predators.

Little brown bats typically fly about 12 miles (20 kilometers) per hour but can go almost twice as fast when needed. Their tiny hearts beat about a thousand times every minute as they fly through the night sky.

When winter approaches, the little brown bat can choose to stay where it is and hibernate or migrate to warmer temperatures and plentiful insects. Hibernating bats' heart rates slow down to about 20 beats a minute, and they can go about 30 minutes without taking a breath.

Few mammals choose how they will survive the winter. Some are designed to hibernate, some to migrate, and others to adapt. But little brown bats choose. God gives us a choice too. Instead of programming people like robots, he lets us decide if we want to live in heaven with him. If you have never done so, you can pray to God right now to ask Jesus into your heart. Ask him to forgive you of your sins, and trust him to take care of you.

Do you have questions about what it means to be saved? Write your questions here and ask an adult to talk about them with you.

If you confess with your mouth that Jesus is Lord and believe in your heart that God raised him from the dead, you will be saved.

ROMANS 10:9

Heavenly Father, I want to live with you forever! I am sorry for the wrong things I've done. Please forgive me for my sins. I know Jesus died on the cross so I can live in heaven someday. I want Jesus to live in my heart. Thank you for loving me. Help me to live for you. In Jesus' name, amen.

Wild Wonder

A baby bat is called a pup.

Creature Connection

Find a friend to do this activity with you. Ask an adult if you can use a ruler and a bandanna or other cloth for a blindfold. With your friend, gather several small (mostly) flat items such as a piece of paper, a piece of aluminum foil, a towel, a clipboard, etc. While you are blindfolded, have your partner place the flat items on the floor around you. Use the ruler to tap around until you find an item. Listen for changes in the taps to identify which item you found—like echolocation. Then switch roles.

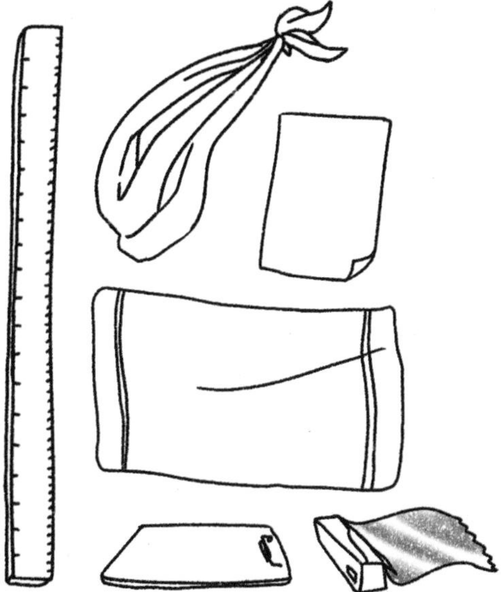

Serval

Scientific Name: *Leptailurus serval*

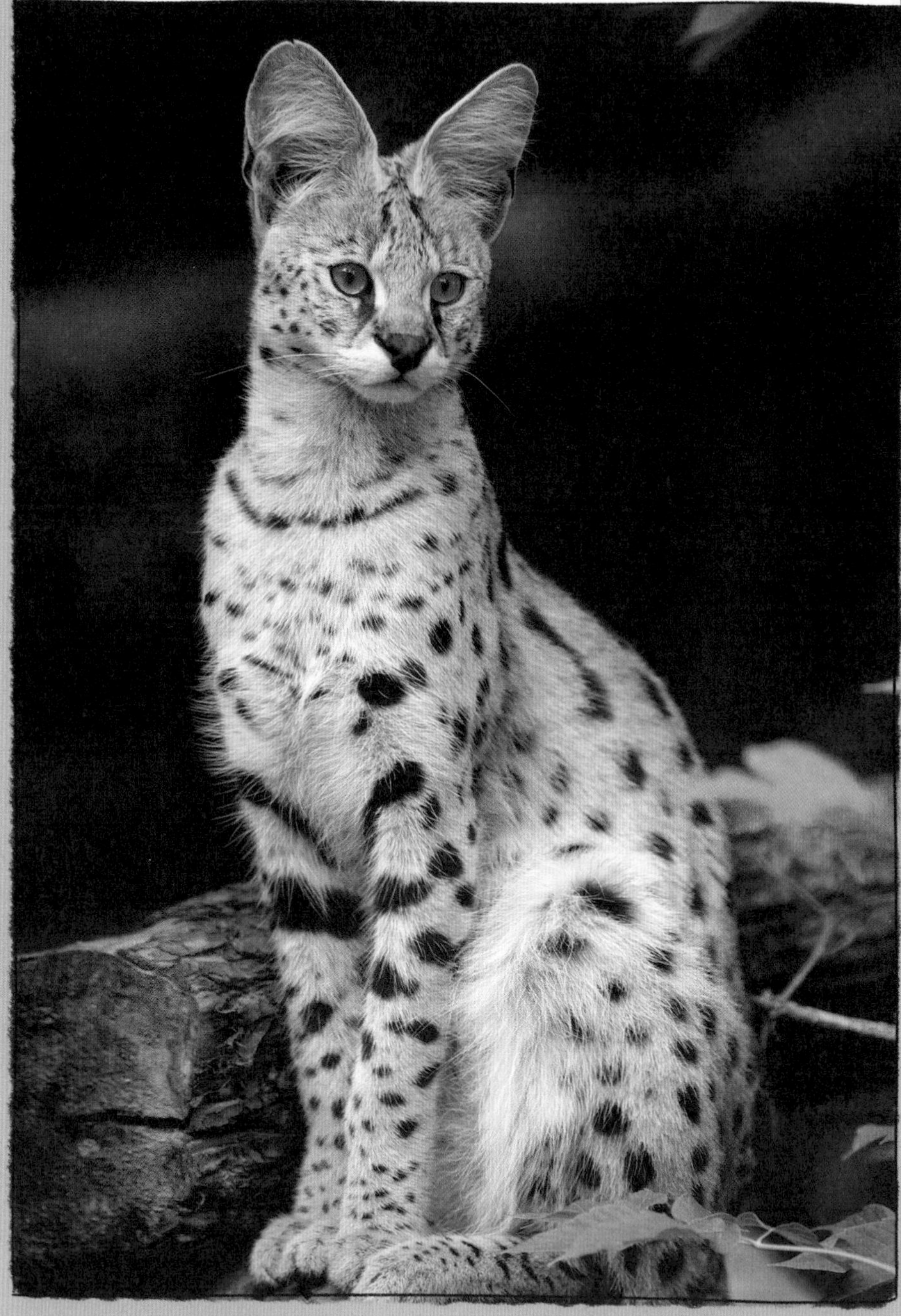

Sneaky Serval

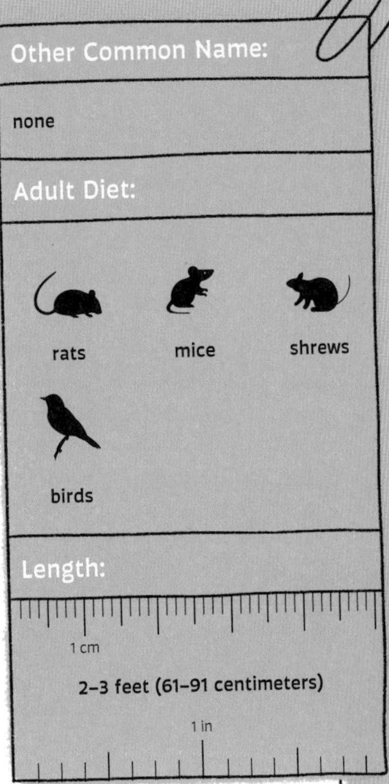

Other Common Name:
none
Adult Diet:
rats
mice
shrews
birds
Length:
1 cm
2–3 feet (61–91 centimeters)
1 in

The long-legged wildcat called the serval lives throughout much of southern Africa. This spotted cat rests during the heat of the day. It hunts in the morning, late afternoon, and at night. The serval scans an area and listens closely, without moving. It concentrates with its eyes closed—for up to 15 minutes.

As the serval listens, its ears rotate in different directions, targeting the prey. And then . . . pounce! With a vertical hop more than 6 feet (2 meters) in the air, the serval's front paws land precisely on its next meal.

Servals are expert hunters and may catch about 15 animals a day. If a rodent burrows underground, the serval digs through the soil to find it. Though rodents make up most of their diet, servals also hunt birds. They pluck the birds they catch before eating them.

The spots on servals' fur camouflage them. When servals are in open areas, they move with stealth to the safety of taller grass.

A serval kitten weighs just 8 ounces (240 grams) at birth. It doubles its size in the first 11 days of life. By 5 months of age, it hunts with its mother. Around the first birthday, the young serval leaves its mother to find its own territory.

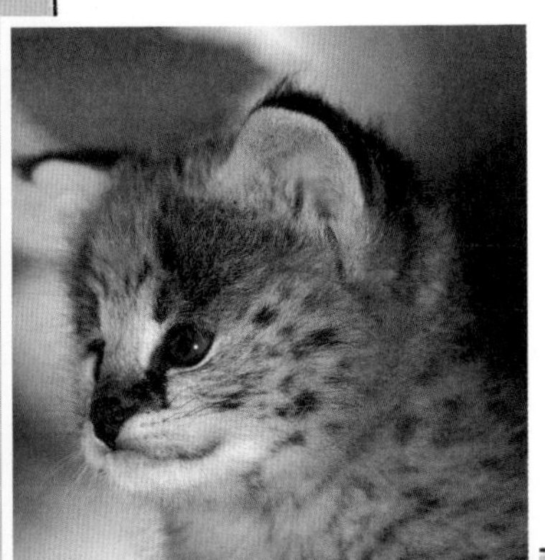

You can learn from your parents and other trusted grown-ups like serval kittens do. Ask why faith is important to them. Watch how they live their lives. Ask them to help you find answers to your big faith questions. Listen to their advice. Thank God for the wisdom they share with you.

Write down some questions you would like to ask an adult about their life and their faith.

Honor your father and your mother, so that you ma live long in the land the Lor your God is giving you.

EXODUS 20:12, NIV

Lord God, thank you for the trustworthy adults in my life. Help me to learn from their faith. In Jesus' name, amen.

Wild Wonder

Unlike most savanna animals, servals usually live by themselves.

Creature Connection

Prepare 5 to 10 questions for an interview with a Christian adult you know and admire. Consider asking them about their faith and how they came to know God. Also ask how they meet the challenges of life and how their faith helps them. Your questions don't have to be all faith related. Ask about their childhood, hobbies, family, and more.

Short-Tailed Chinchilla

Scientific Name: *Chinchilla chinchilla*

The Softest Fur

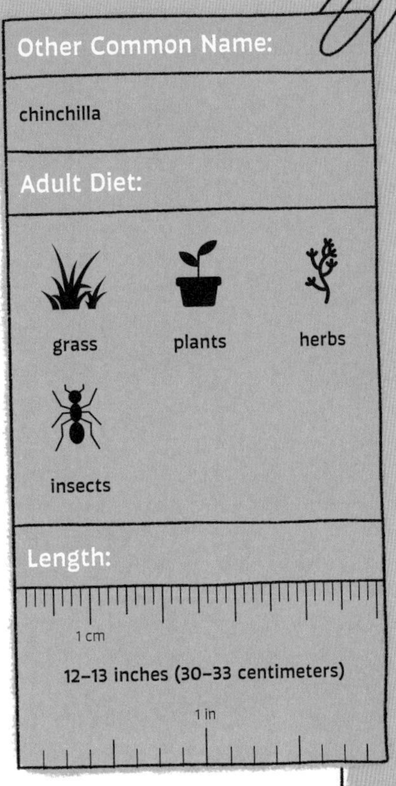

Short-tailed chinchillas make their homes in rock crevices in the Andes Mountains of South America. They live in groups. Some groups are small. Others have more than a hundred chinchillas in them.

Chinchillas bask in the sun at dawn and dusk when they're most active. They feast on any vegetation found in their habitat. When chinchillas eat, they sit on their hind legs and stuff their cheek pouches with herbs and grasses using their front paws.

Chinchillas' feet are designed for climbing and moving on rocks. Their footpads, along with great skill, keep them from slipping when they run and jump among the rocks. Their 4-inch (10-centimeter) whiskers help them navigate in the dark. In tight spaces, the whiskers also let them know if a hole is large enough for them to fit.

Chinchillas weigh 1.2 ounces (35 grams) at birth. That's about the same weight as a small box of raisins. They're born with fur and teeth. Newborn chinchillas climb onto their mother's back for more warmth. Wild populations are rare since chinchillas are endangered. People breed them in captivity for the pet and fur trades.

The fur of chinchillas is considered one of the most valuable furs in the world. It's incredibly soft and thick. God didn't give you soft fur, but he gave you the ability to think and feel. What you watch, read, play, and talk about influences you. Keep your mind open and your heart soft so God can work in your life.

List a few things you like to read, watch, and talk about with your friends. Draw a heart by those that make your heart soft toward God.

Open my eyes that I may see wonderful things in your law.

PSALM 119:18, NIV

Jesus, thank you for softening my heart so I can know you more. In your name, amen.

Wild Wonder

Short-tailed chinchillas have been hunted for their fur to the point of near extinction.

Creature Connection

Collect a small rock from your yard or neighborhood. Use a marker to draw eyes, nose, ears, and a tail. Then glue a soft piece of felt, fabric, or a pom-pom to the rock to remind you of the chinchilla's soft fur and how God wants you to keep your heart soft toward him.

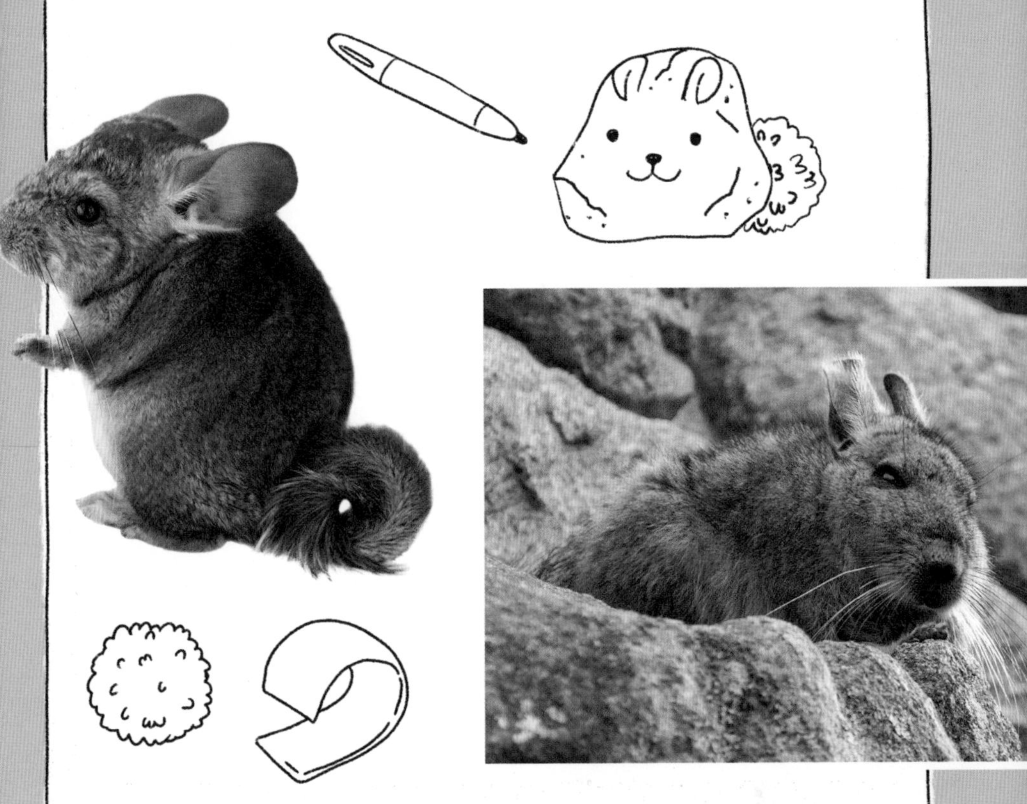

In the Wild

The next time you see big rocks or boulders, ask an adult for permission to climb on them. Do you climb using just your feet, or do you also use your hands? Use caution since your legs, feet, and shoes aren't designed the same way a chinchilla's legs, feet, and footpads are.

Hoffmann's Two-Toed Sloth

Scientific Name: *Choloepus hoffmanni*

Sloth Stealth

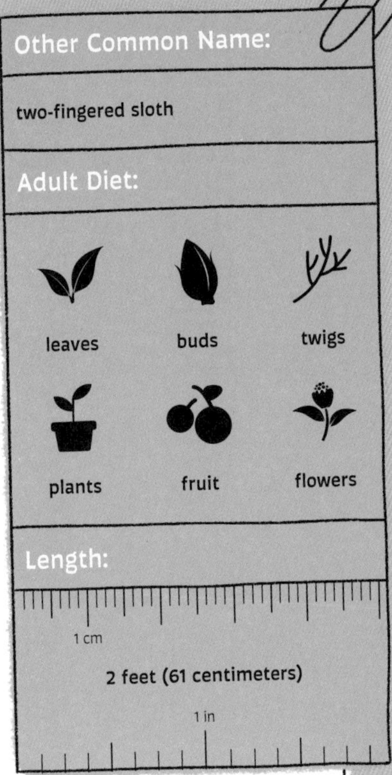

In the tropical forests of Central and South America, the Hoffmann's two-toed sloth eats, sleeps, and even gives birth hanging from tree limbs. It tilts its head wayyyyy back to watch for danger and tasty plants.

Sloths digest slowly as leaves move through their 4-chambered stomachs. Since two-toed sloths consume just 100 to 150 calories per day (about as much as a snack bag of potato chips), they must save their energy.

Sloths appear to sleep all day. However, they only *look* like they're asleep. With eyes closed, sloths are completely inactive but awake most of the time. New research shows sloths only sleep 8 to 10 hours a day.

Two-toed sloths hide to survive; they cannot run. They move so slowly, prey don't notice them. It's not laziness; it's sloth stealth mode. During the rainy season, rain drips off the two-toed sloths, and algae grow on their fur. The algae give them even more protection in the form of camouflage.

Little movement is part of sloths' design. God knows these slow movers are an important part of their environment. You might be a fast talker, a competitive game player, or a daydreamer. You may not understand your personality, but God knows why he made you this way. Look for the good in all your traits and know God does too.

Write down the personality traits you like best about yourself. How can you use them for God?

Two Toes?

All sloths have three toes on their hind legs. The Hoffmann two-toed sloth's front limbs are different with two toes on each. Other sloths have three toes on their front limbs.

Let your adorning be the hidden person of the heart with the imperishable beauty of a gentle and quiet spirit, which in God's sight is very precious.

1 PETER 3:4

Heavenly Father, thank you for reminding me that you love me just as I am. In Jesus' name, amen.

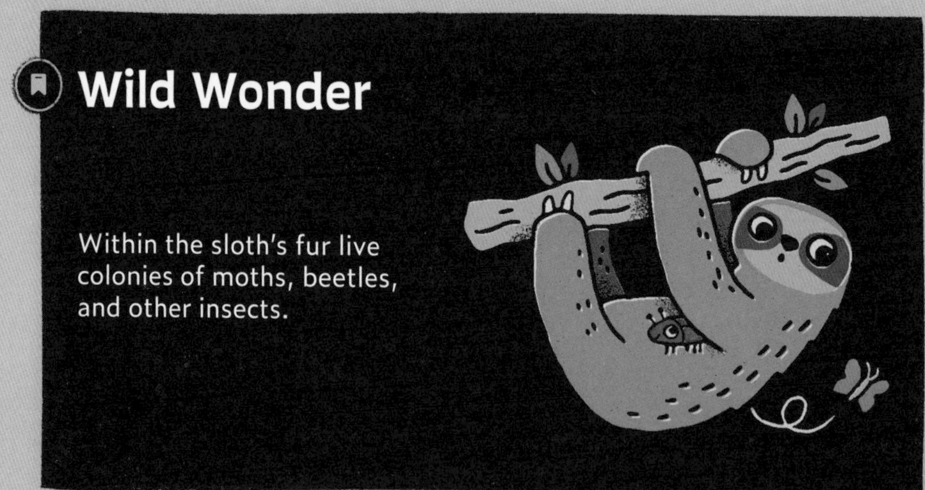

Wild Wonder

Within the sloth's fur live colonies of moths, beetles, and other insects.

Creature Connection

Draw a tree on a piece of construction paper. Write a feature of your personality along each of the branches of the tree. If you like, include a sloth hanging from one of the branches!

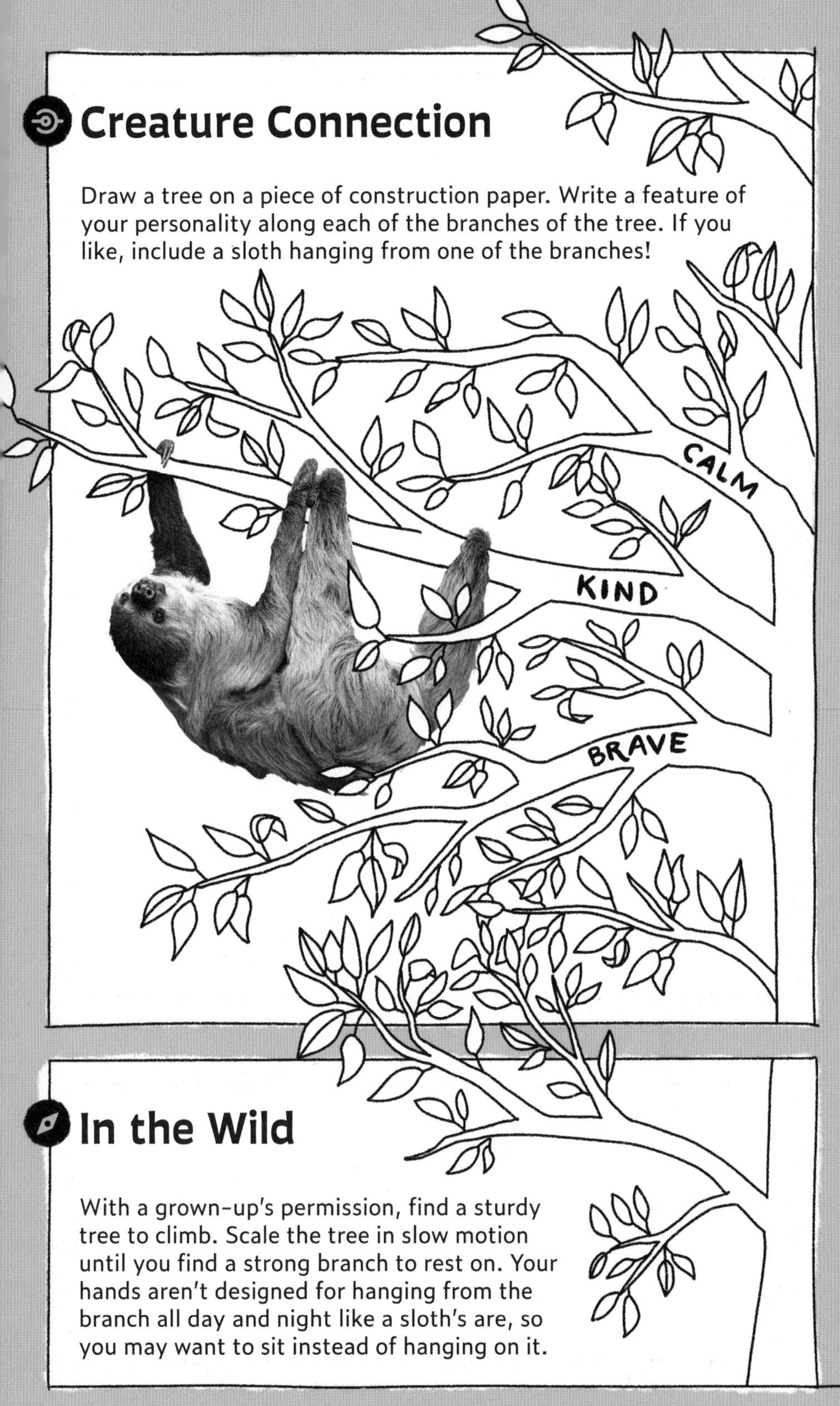

In the Wild

With a grown-up's permission, find a sturdy tree to climb. Scale the tree in slow motion until you find a strong branch to rest on. Your hands aren't designed for hanging from the branch all day and night like a sloth's are, so you may want to sit instead of hanging on it.

Bottlenose Dolphin

Scientific Name: *Tursiops truncatus*

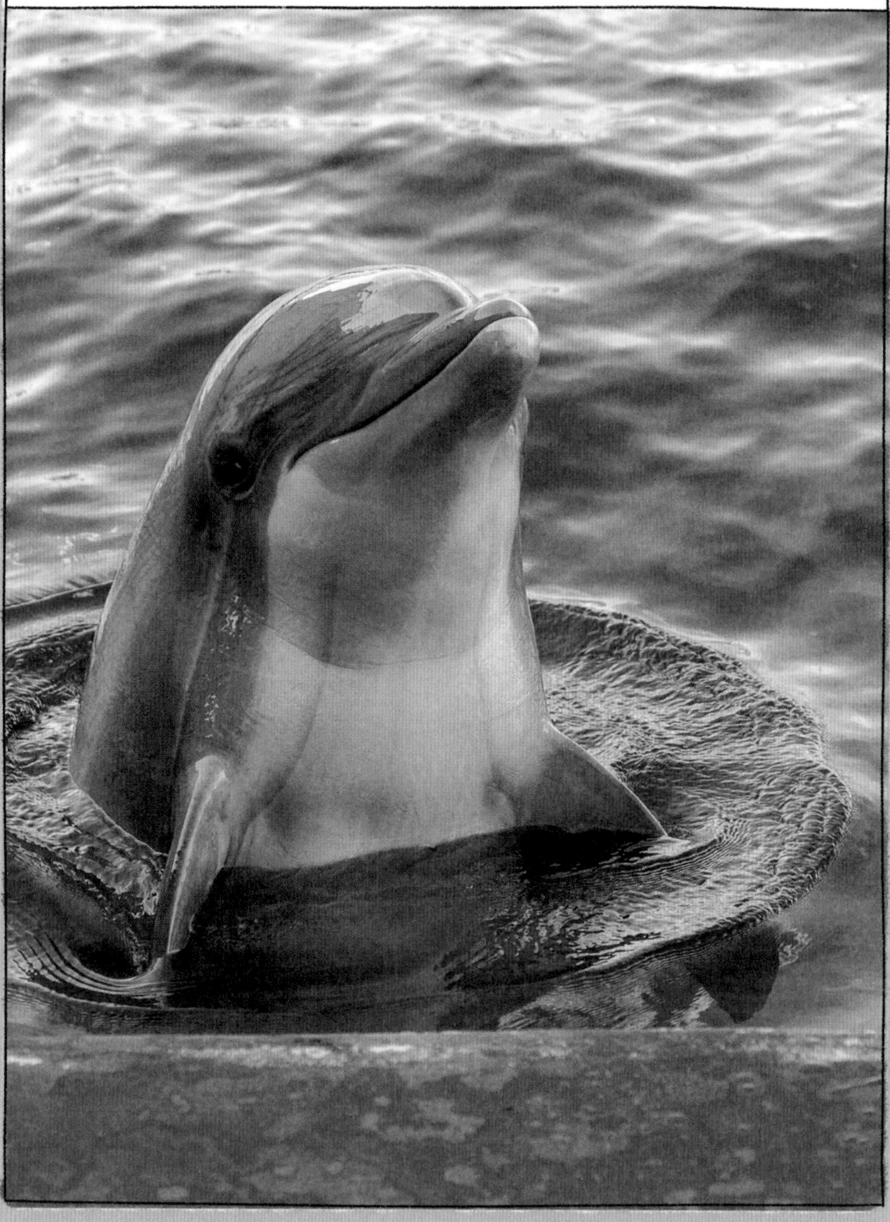

Body Talk

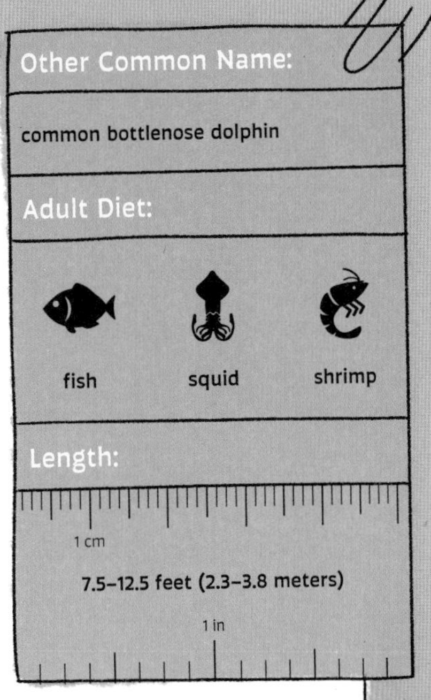

Other Common Name:
common bottlenose dolphin
Adult Diet:
fish
squid
shrimp
Length:
1 cm
7.5–12.5 feet (2.3–3.8 meters)
1 in

Needing to fill their lungs with air, bottlenose dolphins surface as frequently as a couple of times each minute. They live in oceans everywhere except the polar waters. Bottlenose dolphins can swim as fast as 18 miles (29 kilometers) per hour, but they typically go about as fast as you walk.

Bottlenose dolphins are social animals, so they live in groups called pods. Some groups are small, with just a few dolphins, but other pods have more than a hundred. The dolphins form relationships that can last decades, and dolphins can live more than 50 years.

Dolphins are intelligent animals. They solve problems in the wild as well as in captivity with trainers conducting experiments. They also like to play and have fun.

In addition to their great eyesight, dolphins have excellent hearing. They use echolocation to tell the shape, size, and location of an underwater object. When their high-frequency clicking sounds hit something, the sound bounces off and returns to the dolphin as an echo.

Dolphins can communicate through body language. Their bodies "talk" with snapping of jaws, leaping in the air (up to 20 feet or 6 meters), blowing bubbles, butting heads, and slapping their tails on the water. Dolphins even "talk" with sounds. They squeak and squawk, and every dolphin develops a unique whistle that their group members recognize. The whistle can share their location.

Just as bottlenose dolphins effectively communicate with one another, we should talk to God through prayer. It's how we build a relationship with our heavenly Father. He also gave us the Holy Spirit, who prays for us when we don't know how to pray. Talk to God today.

What are some things you'd like to pray about? Write them down and pray for the items on your list every day this week.

The Spirit helps us in our weakness. We do not know what we ought to pray for, but the Spirit himself intercedes for us through wordless groans.

ROMANS 8:26, NIV

Holy Spirit, thank you for praying for me when I don't have the words to pray. In Jesus' name, amen.

Wild Wonder

Bottlenose dolphins shed their skin every 2 hours.

Creature Connection

With an adult's permission, use the Internet to see dolphins in action. You might watch a video or find a webcam online. Do some additional research to learn more about dolphins. Which kind of dolphin is the largest of all? Where can some dolphin species live other than the ocean?

Scientists estimate there are millions of insect species, and at any time there may be

10 quintillion

(10,000,000,000,000,000,000)

individual insects alive. They live on every continent—including Antarctica.

Insects can be microscopic or larger than this book. All adult insects have three body parts (head, thorax, and abdomen) and six legs. Their hard skin is called an exoskeleton.

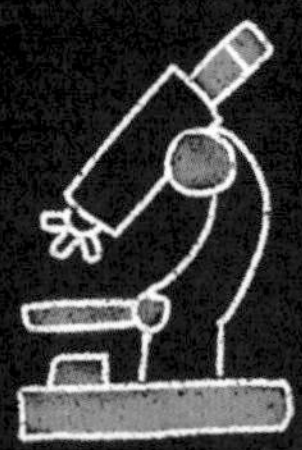

INSECTS

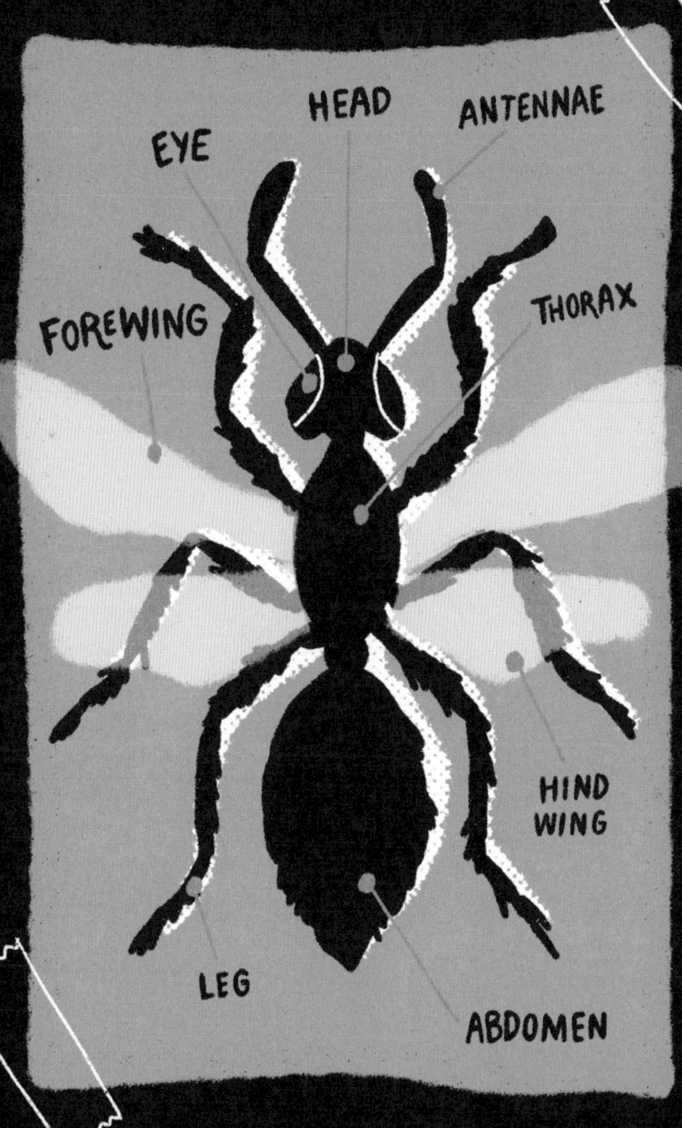

Katydid

Scientific Names: *Orchelimum vulgare*, *Microcentrum rhombifolium*, *Siliquofera grandis*, and more

Creative Differences

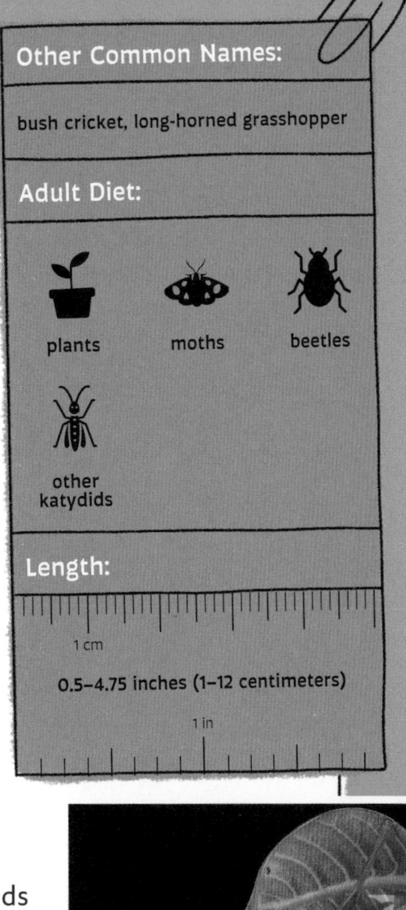

About 6,000 unique kinds of katydids live around the world, making their homes in a variety of climates, such as rain forests and deserts. There are a lot of differences among them. Many katydids are bright green with leaf-like markings. Brown katydids look like dead leaves. Still others are pink or yellow. But they all blend in with their environment.

Even the size of katydids varies greatly. The smallest adults are about the size of your thumbnail, but the predatory bush cricket (a katydid, despite its name) grows to be nearly the length of your hand!

Some katydid species have itty-bitty wings. But the *Siliquofera grandis* has a wingspan of nearly 10 inches (25 centimeters). No matter their wing size, katydids don't fly very well. Instead, they use their wings to propel themselves forward as they jump.

Katydids vary from species to species, but they're all katydids. The differences in katydids show off God's creativity. With over 8 billion people on Earth, you'll meet others who look, talk, and act differently from you. You'll even know people with beliefs unlike your own. God wants us to be respectful and kind to *all* people—not just the ones who seem like us. Think about the people in your school and neighborhood who are different from you. Think about what you have in common and try to make a new friend.

Is there someone new at church, school, or in your neighborhood God might want you to befriend? Write their name(s) here and some ideas on how you could get to know them.

From one man [God] made all the nations, that they should inhabit the whole earth.

ACTS 17:26, NIV

Jesus, help me to love others regardless of our differences, in the same way you love me. In your name, amen.

Wild Wonder

Katydids rub their wings together to make their rasping sounds.

Creature Connection

Find a leaf shaped like an oval. (A few options of trees with oval leaves are elm, ash, or black cherry.) Place the leaf face down so the veins show. Cover it with a plain piece of paper. Make several leaf rubbings using the sides of crayons in different colors to remind you of all the different types of people God has created. Transform your colorful leaf rubbings into katydids by drawing head, legs, and antennae. Camouflage them with more leaf rubbings.

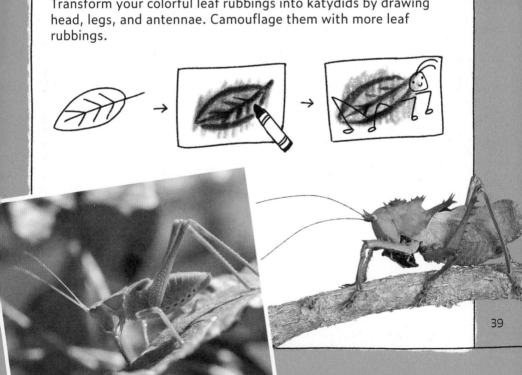

Praying Mantis

Scientific Names: *Mantis religiosa*, *Stagmomantis carolina*, and more

Praying or Preying?

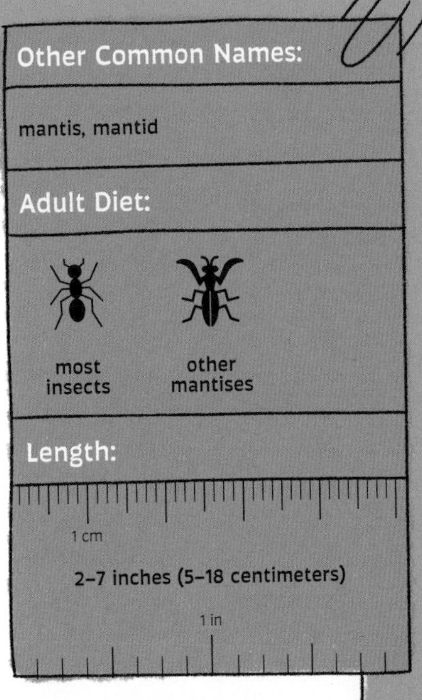

Other Common Names:
mantis, mantid
Adult Diet:
most insects
other mantises
Length:
1 cm
2–7 inches (5–18 centimeters)
1 in

Praying mantises don't hunt down a meal. Instead, they wait for their prey. Their green or brown skin blends in well with bushes and trees. Camouflaged, they sit and wait. The praying mantis watches with five eyes—two bulging compound eyes (made of thousands of mini eyes) and three simple eyes. What does it look for? Dinner.

Praying mantises typically prey on a variety of insects like beetles, butterflies, grasshoppers, and flies. They're not too picky; they even eat hummingbirds, frogs, lizards, and other mantises.

The mantis sits. The prey comes close.

The mantis waits. The prey comes closer.

The mantis strikes.

With a quick, viselike grip, the mantis grabs its prey and holds the meal while it eats.

More than two thousand kinds—or species—of mantises may look like they're praying to God with folded hands, but their posture has nothing to do with worship. They're really preying on other animals. It's easy to bow your head and fold your hands, but prayer is really about talking to God—even silently. We might act like we're praying, but we can't deceive God if we're not sincere. He knows our hearts. He wants you to talk to him because you love him, not because others are listening. Pray to God when you're by yourself—not just with family or a church group. Spend a few minutes right now praying to God.

Write a prayer of worship, thanking God for all he is and all he does for you.

When you pray, go into your room and shut the doo and pray to your Father who is in secret. And your Father who sees in secret will reward you.

MATTHEW 6:6

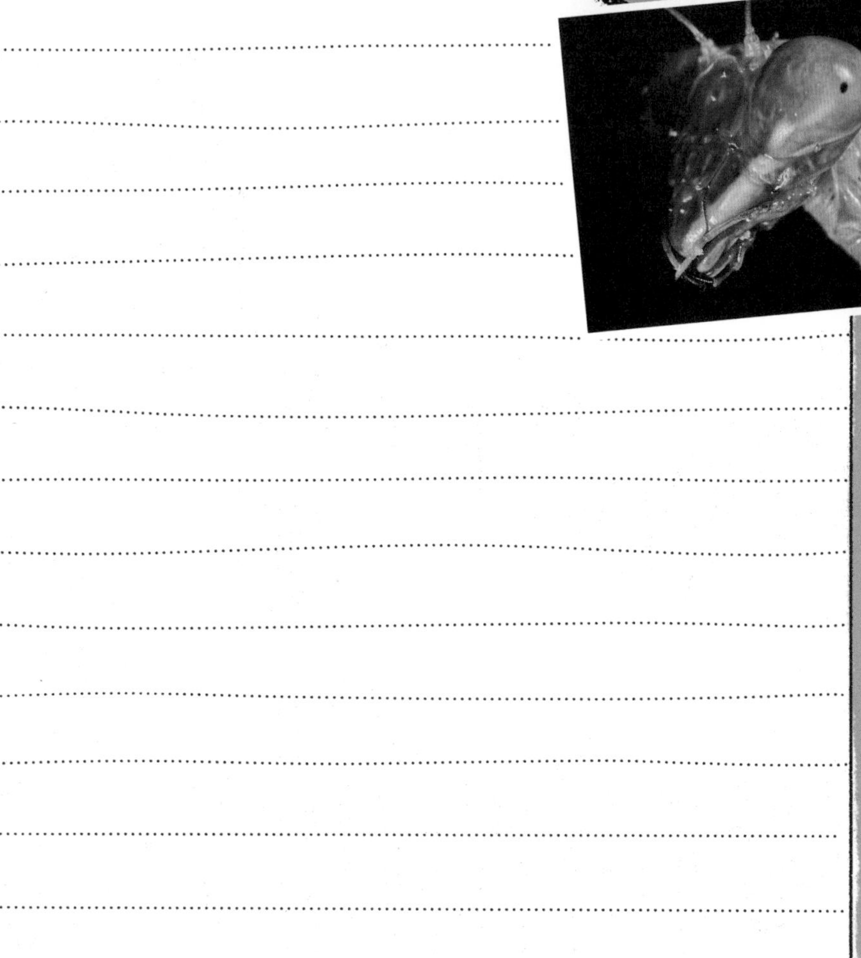

Lord God, you are worthy of all praise and prayers. I love you. In Jesus' name, amen.

Wild Wonder

Praying mantises can turn their heads to either side 180 degrees and see in all directions.

Creature Connection

Make a praying mantis craft as a reminder to pray. Cut a triangle from green paper. Turn the paper so one point is at the bottom. Use a marker to add large eyes to the top corners. Draw a V-shaped mouth in the bottom corner and add two antennae using glue or tape. (You can use pipe cleaners or strips of green paper for your antennae.) Place the praying mantis near your bed as a reminder to start and end each day with prayer.

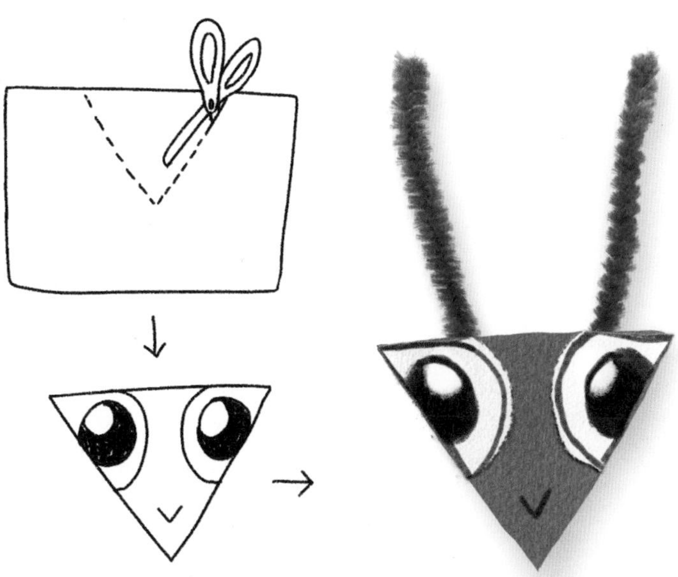

Honey Bee

Scientific Name: *Apis mellifera*

A Buzzy Team

Honey bees live as a group called a colony. Each bee has a job to do, but together the honey bees work as a team to help the colony survive.

Female worker bees make up most of the colony. Worker bees' jobs are based on their age. Some clean or guard the hive. Nursery workers feed larvae—the immature wormlike form of the bees. The honey bees we see buzzing around forage for flower nectar and pollen. The collected food feeds 50,000 bees that live in their colony.

Other Common Name:

honeybee

Adult Diet:

nectar pollen honey

Length:

1 cm

0.5–0.75 inch (1–2 centimeters)

1 in

There are only a few drones, or male honey bees, in each colony, but they have an important task. They mate with the queen outside the hive. After they finish this one job, they die.

Each colony has only one queen. She lays more than 1,000 eggs each day—about an egg every minute! She doesn't have time or energy to feed or clean herself. The worker bees care for all the queen bee's needs. The honey bee does what is best for the colony without being asked.

We work in groups in activities, at school, and even at home. When we don't do our tasks, others must do their work and ours. What can you do today to help your family, team, or classmates? Can you set the table for dinner before the meal is ready? Can you tidy up your classroom floor? Our work honors God.

Make a list of ways you can be like a honey bee, serving your family, friends, and others around you. Then go do some of them!

Do nothing from selfish ambition or conceit, but in humility count others more significant than yourselves. Let each of you look not only to his own interests, but also to the interests of others.

PHILIPPIANS 2:3-4

Heavenly Father, thank you for the groups I'm part of. Help me work hard in all I do and support others. In Jesus' name, amen.

Wild Wonders

Honey bees are so hairy, even their eyes have hair.

Creature Connection

Prepare a honey snack for your family. Make a slice of toast for each family member. Spread butter on each slice and then drizzle on a bit of honey. Serve warm.

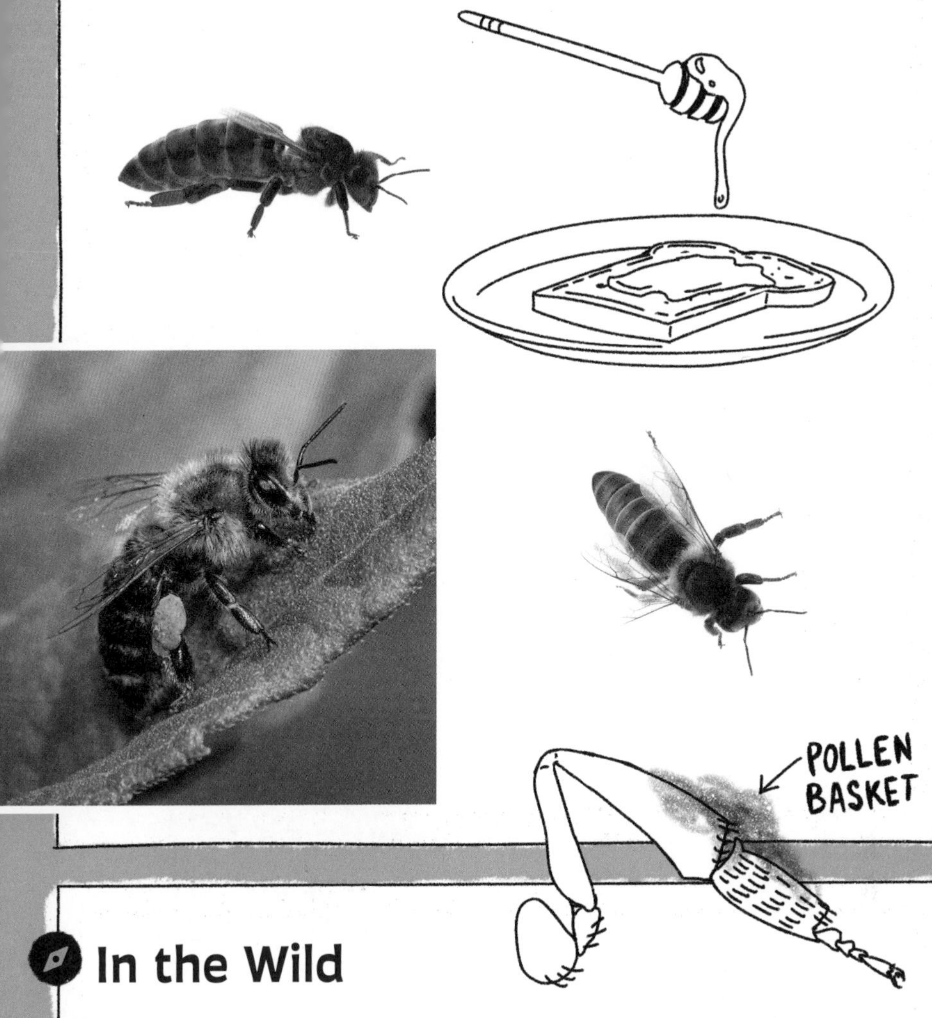

In the Wild

Go outside where you can observe honey bees (or other bees) during the spring or summer. Count how many flowers a bee visits in a minute. As long as you aren't allergic to bee stings, try to get extra close to a bee. (Honey bees rarely sting since they die if they sting you.) See if you can spot pollen baskets on the hind legs of the honey bee. They'll look like yellow blobs.

Hercules Beetle

Scientific Name: *Dynastes hercules*

Super Strength

The horns of the male Hercules beetle can grow even longer than its body, making the beetle nearly 7 inches (18 centimeters) from end to end. It's long—and strong.

Hercules beetles live on forest floors, especially in rain forests. They have two sets of wings. Their outer wings are hard. They protect the wings underneath that give the giant beetles flight. Different kinds of Hercules beetles have wings in different colors, like black, brown, green, yellow, blue, and white.

This huge, nocturnal insect doesn't hunt down other animals with its giant horns and massive strength. Instead, it eats fruit that has fallen on the ground. But sometimes the horns come in handy.

A male Hercules beetle challenges another male. They fight over a female. One uses its horns like a claw against an opponent. First, he grabs the other beetle between the horns. He lifts it and then throws the rival to the ground. They keep fighting until one is injured or leaves. Then the winner gets to mate with the female.

Hercules beetles are strong—so strong that they can carry 100 times their weight. That's like an 80-pound (36-kilogram) kid lifting 4 tons (3.5 metric tons)! When we understand we're weak without God, he helps us. God promises to give us strength. His strength comes in the form of courage, patience, or physical endurance when we are tired.

What do you need help with? Pray today and ask God to give you strength. Rely on him in this hard situation. God can help you find a friend, be patient with your sister, and so much more.

Can you think of some ways to "exercise" spiritually? Write them down and work on adding one new activity to your time with God each week.

The LORD is my strength and my shield; in him my heart trusts, and I am helped.

PSALM 28:7

Lord, help me to remember all my strength comes from you. In Jesus' name, amen.

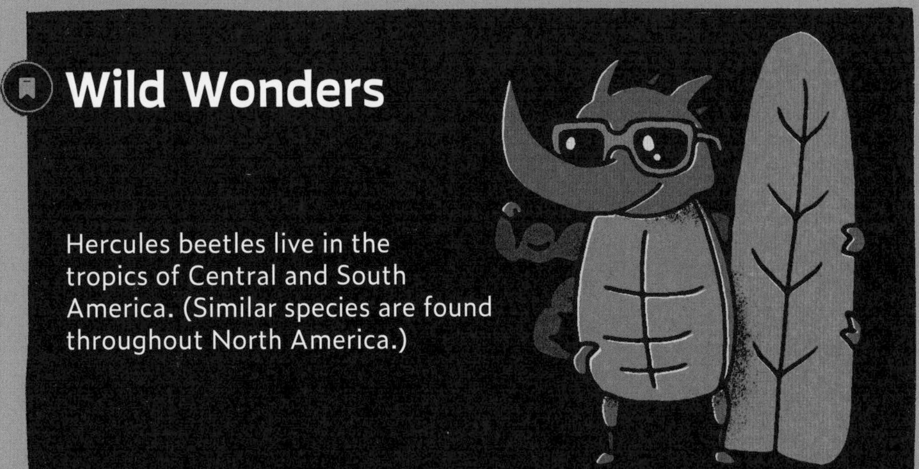

Wild Wonders

Hercules beetles live in the tropics of Central and South America. (Similar species are found throughout North America.)

Creature Connection

Keep your brain and body strong with exercise. Choose an exercise you want to learn or master, such as a push-up, burpee, or jumping jack. With an adult's permission, search online for a video or ask someone to model the proper form of the exercise. Complete the exercises. Count repetitions until you notice your muscles tiring. Do the exercise each day for a week, adding more repetitions. You're stronger already!

Firefly

Scientific Names: *Photinus pyralis*, *Photuris frontalis*, and more

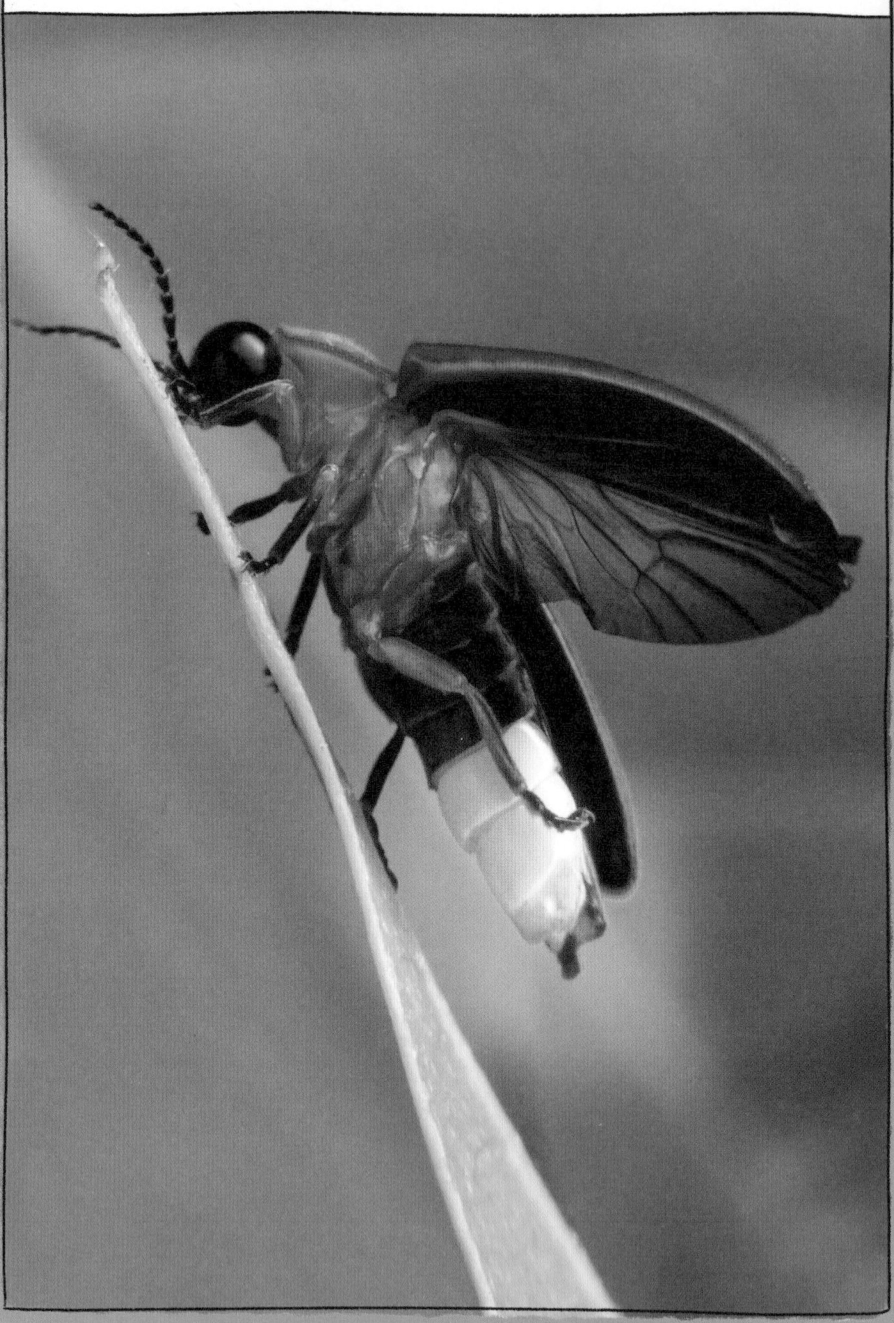

Living Lights

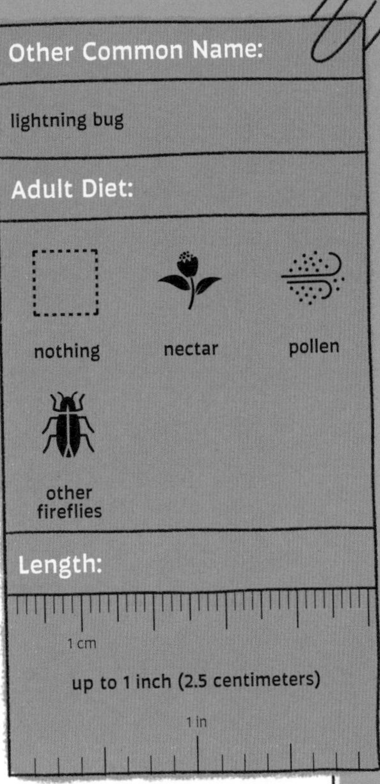

Other Common Name:
lightning bug
Adult Diet:
nothing
nectar
pollen
other fireflies
Length:
1 cm
up to 1 inch (2.5 centimeters)
1 in

Blinking lights add magic to summer nights. Those flashing lights are winged beetles. They're fireflies—or you might call them lightning bugs.

Each firefly has a see-through tail called a lantern. Chemicals fill the lantern. The firefly uses tubes called tracheoles to get oxygen from the air. Then, when the firefly's chemicals and oxygen mix, the lantern glows with light.

Since they can't talk, fireflies use their lights to communicate. Their lights might say, "Look at me! I'd make a great mate." Other times fireflies flash their lights to say, "Warning! Don't eat me. I taste nasty."

Scientists have a name for the light that comes from some living things like plants, animals, and bacteria. It's called bio-luminescence. It means *life light*.

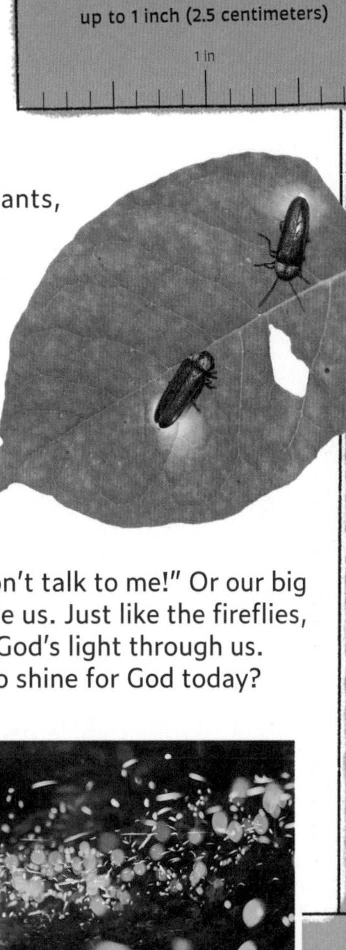

God created fireflies and people to shine his brilliance. We don't typically use lights to communicate with others. Instead, we use our words and actions. The way we talk to friends and family *and* what we do tells them about God's goodness.

If we cross our arms, it's like shouting, "Don't talk to me!" Or our big grin can invite a new classmate to sit beside us. Just like the fireflies, our light is meant to be life light—shining God's light through us. How will you use your words and actions to shine for God today?

List some words and actions that would show other people God's goodness through you.

Let your light shine before others, so that they may see your good works and give glory to your Father who is in heaven.

MATTHEW 5:16

God, help me to shine brightly for you today, showing others your love through my actions. In Jesus' name, amen.

Wild Wonders

Some species of fireflies don't flash, but they're still part of the firefly family.

Creature Connection

With a friend, learn Morse code from a book or online search. (Check with an adult before using the Internet.) Then send each other messages using flashlights at night or by tapping them out on a hard surface.

In the Wild

On a summer night, watch fireflies in action. See if you can track one firefly long enough to figure out its flashing pattern. Then use your hands to scoop up the firefly. Place it in a jar with air holes so you can observe it. Keep the jar moist with damp grass or a wet paper towel. Release the firefly after a few hours.

Blue Death-Feigning Beetle

Scientific Name: *Asbolus verrucosus*

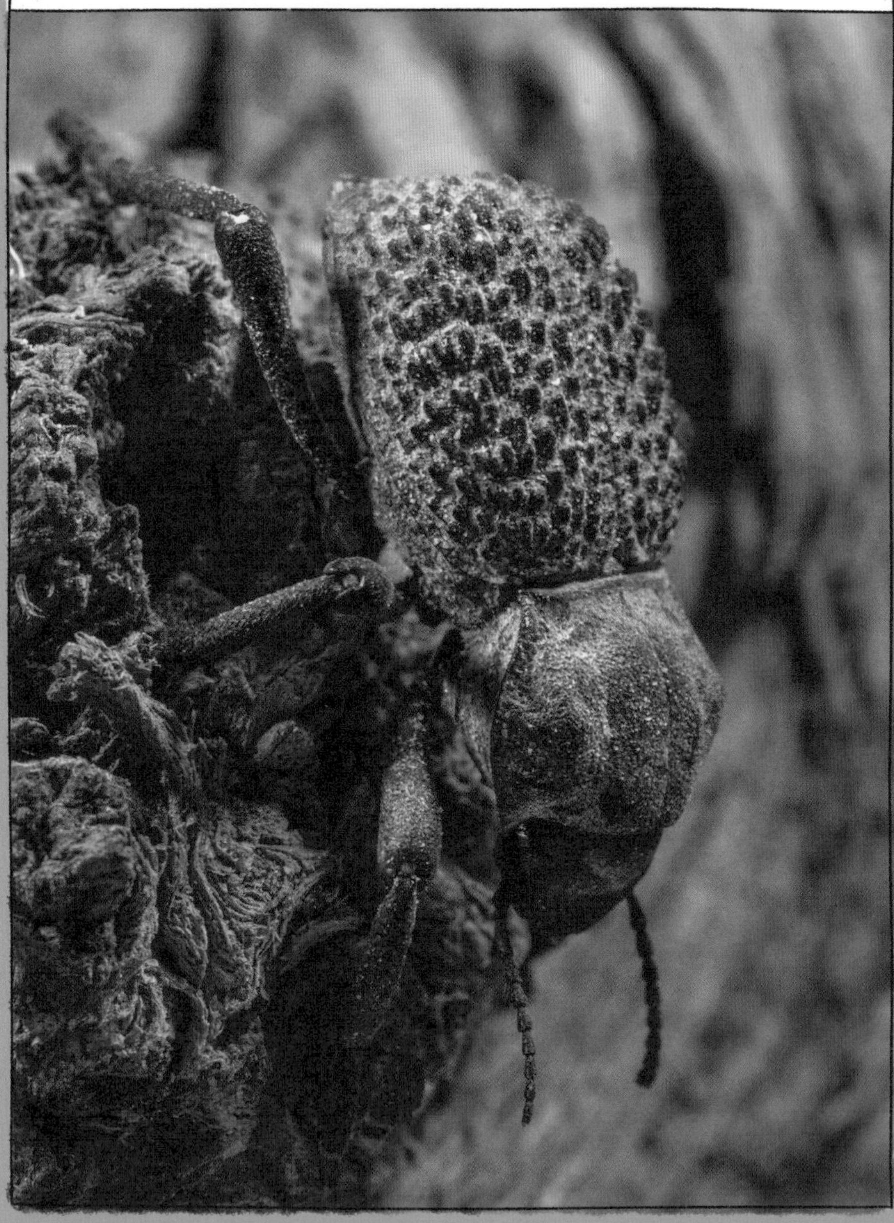

Feeling Blue

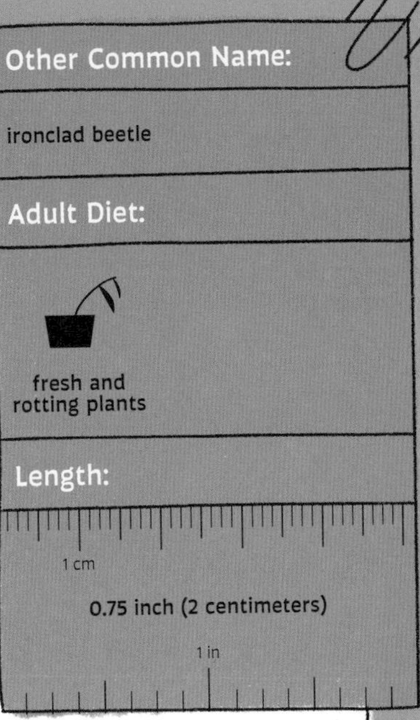

Other Common Name:
ironclad beetle
Adult Diet:
fresh and rotting plants
Length:
1 cm
0.75 inch (2 centimeters)
1 in

What a name! But the blue death-feigning beetles' name describes them perfectly. First, they are blue. And second, these beetles play dead (death-feigning) to protect themselves. When threatened, these beetles roll over with their legs in the air. They don't move until they feel safe again. Faking death helps the beetles since predators have a hard time spotting them if the blue death-feigning beetles aren't moving. Plus, playing dead helps the beetles live longer because most predators want to eat a fresh meal—not an animal that may be dead.

These amazing beetles live in the deserts of the southwestern United States. It doesn't rain much in the desert. So how do the blue death-feigning beetles survive without much water? Their color gives us a clue.

Thick blue wax covers the blue death-feigning beetle. The wax helps it keep water inside its body. If a blue death-feigning beetle gets wet, the wax disappears! The wax returns when the beetle dries out again. The beetle is only covered in wax when it needs to conserve water.

Just as the wax keeps needed moisture in the blue death-feigning beetle's body, we need God's truth with us to keep us walking closely with him. How can we do this? When we memorize verses of the Bible, we have God's Word with us and *in* us—even if no actual Bible is nearby. For the next week, challenge yourself to memorize a verse or passage from the Bible. Tell your family your goal so they can help you.

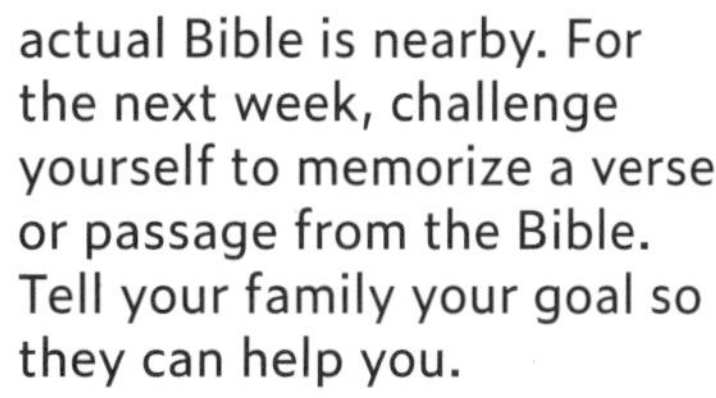

Pick a Bible verse or passage you'd like to memorize. Write it here so you can test your knowledge every day.

I have hidden your word in my heart that I might not sin against you.

PSALM 119:11, NIV

Holy Spirit, guide me and nudge me to commit to keeping God's Word in my heart and mind. In Jesus' name, amen.

Wild Wonders

Blue death-feigning beetles are the prey of spiders.

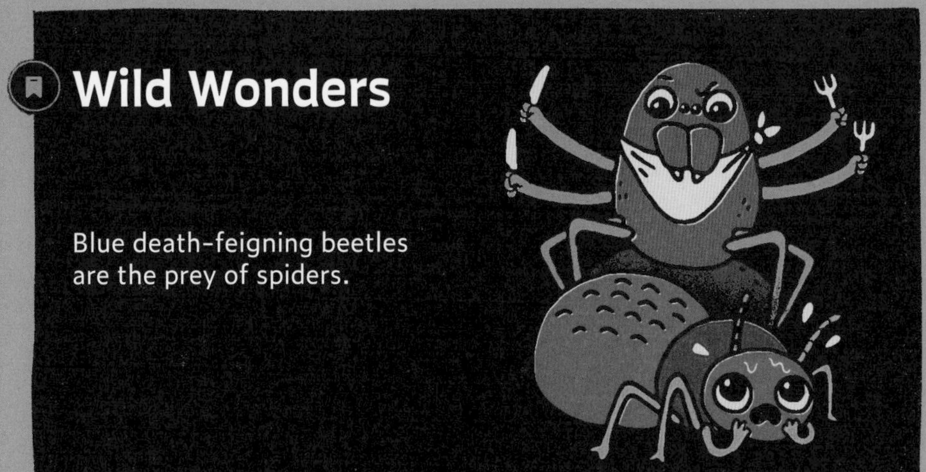

Creature Connection

On white paper, use a white crayon to write your favorite Bible verse or draw a picture that reminds you of God. Your verse will be invisible—until you use watercolor paints to color over the entire page. The crayon wax protects your paper from absorbing the watercolor!

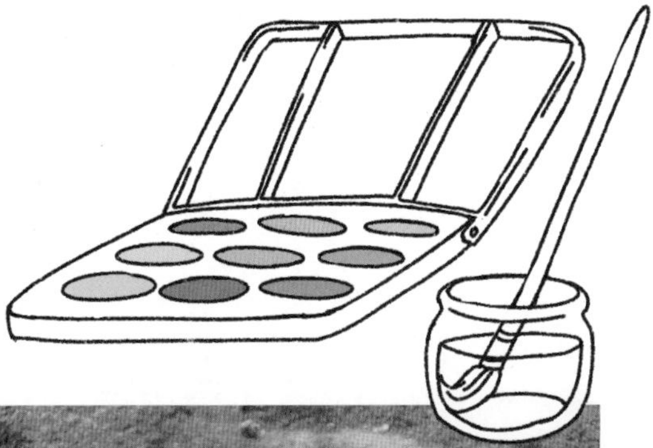

Monarch Butterfly

Scientific Name: *Danaus plexippus*

Heavenly Home

Every fall, monarch butterflies disappear from Canada and colder regions of the United States. Like birds, they migrate, flying south for the winter.

The monarchs leave their summer breeding grounds and fly during the day. They roost in trees with thick leaf canopies at night. In the morning, the butterflies feed on flower nectar and warm themselves in the sunshine. Then they continue their journey.

Other Common Name:

none, but commonly confused with the viceroy butterfly

Adult Diet:

flower nectar

Length:

1 cm

3.5–5 inches (9–13 centimeters)

1 in

The monarchs from the eastern parts of North America travel as many as 3,000 miles (4,800 kilometers) south to the Sierra Madre mountains. Once there, the butterflies cluster on oyamel fir trees in giant colonies. Groups have numbered more than a million. The monarchs from the western parts of North America overwinter in California's Monterey pines and Monterey cypress trees. But they only stay until it starts to get warmer. Then they fly to their summer grounds, laying eggs on milkweed plants along the way. These eggs become new generations of monarchs that continue the journey.

Monarchs instinctively know how to find their way to their northern home. Here on earth, we have a temporary home, but God has a home prepared for all believers in heaven when we die. You know you're ready for heaven if you have given your heart and life to Jesus. You will be reunited with family and friends and meet Jesus! Tell God today what you most look forward to about heaven.

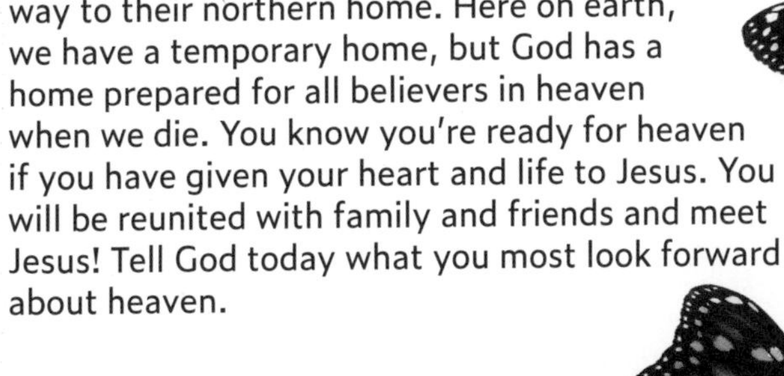

Who are some people you look forward to seeing in heaven? What are you hoping to do when you are there? Jot down some thoughts below.

In my Father's house are many rooms. If it were not so, would I have told you that I go to prepare a place for you?

JOHN 14:2

Dear God, thank you for giving me a home with you in heaven where I will never feel lonely or sad again. In Jesus' name, amen.

Wild Wonder

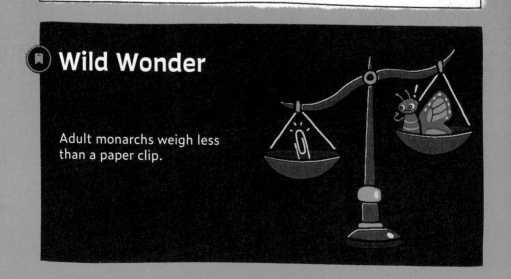

Adult monarchs weigh less than a paper clip.

Creature Connection

The monarch is just one of God's creatures that needs our help because it is threatened with extinction. Some scientists even list the monarch as endangered. Be a citizen scientist and help researchers track monarchs. Visit journeynorth.org/monarchs to learn how you can look for and report your sightings of monarch eggs, caterpillars, and adults.

In the Wild

In the summer and early fall, look for monarch eggs, caterpillars, or chrysalises on milkweed plants.

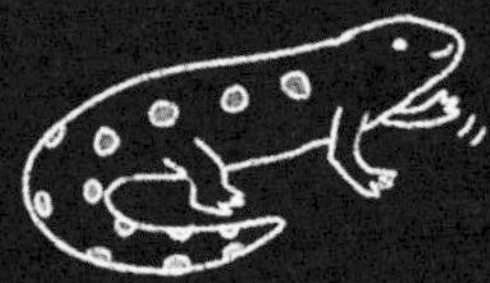

Scientists classify amphibians into 3 groups: frogs (which includes toads), salamanders, and earthworm-like creatures (but bigger) called caecilians. Scientists identify more than **100** new species of amphibians each year, with nearly **9,000** in total. (About **90** percent of all amphibians are frogs.)

Amphibians hatch from eggs. Though there are exceptions, most amphibians go through a change called metamorphosis, in which their bodies change dramatically.

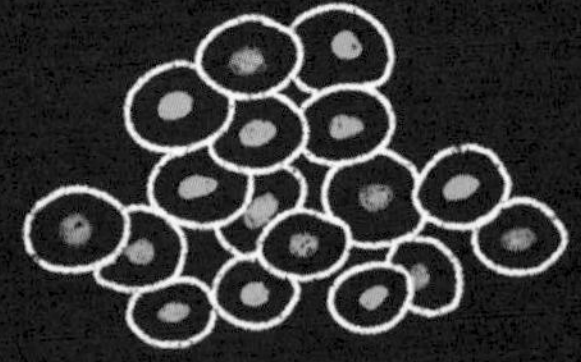

AMPHIBIANS

In the pages that follow, the length of these amphibians does not include the animals' tails. Scientists measure amphibians from their snout (nose) to vent (the opening near their tails used to remove waste).

Wood Frog

Scientific Name: *Lithobates sylvaticus*

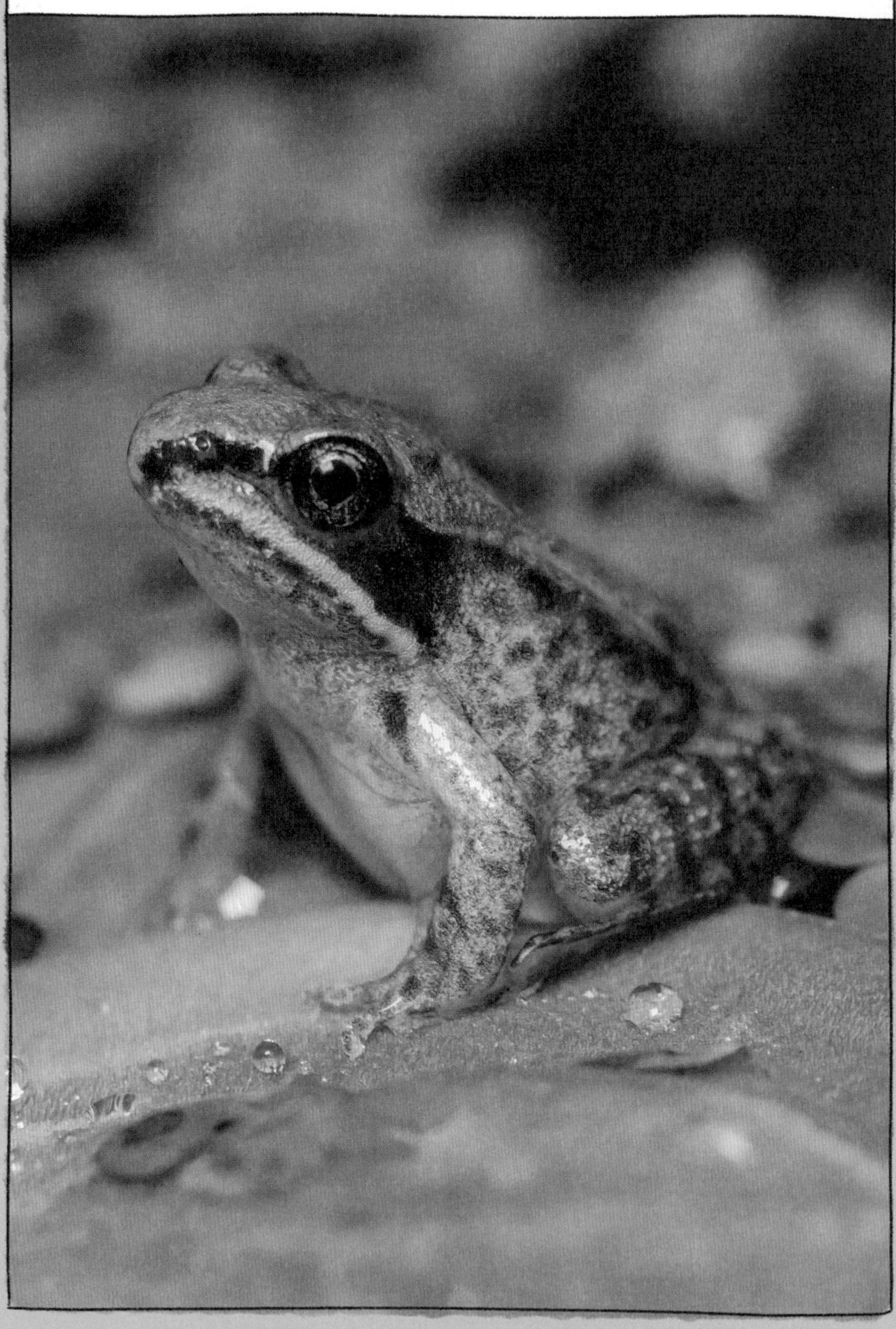

Quack Says the Frog

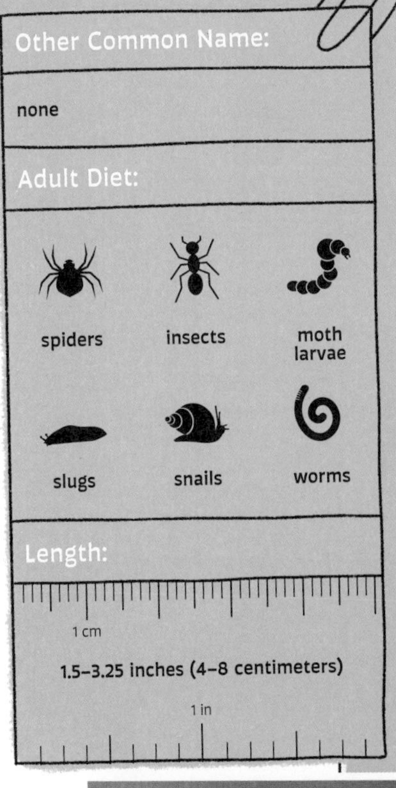

The mating calls of wood frogs are an early sign of spring. These calls aren't particularly loud, but they are distinct.

If you approach a pond or temporary pool, you might hear a lot of quacking—without a duck in sight. The noise may be a group of wood frogs. Once the frogs notice an intruder (like you), they stop calling to their potential mates until they think it's safe again.

To hear and see wood frogs up close, sit or stand very still at the edge of the pond. Watch closely because their brown, black, and pinkish coloring helps them to blend in with the muddy and leaf-filled ponds they prefer for breeding sites.

Nature sounds, like quacking frogs, can fool us, so we should look for the source to know what makes the noise. If someone tells us something and suggests that it's from the Bible, then we should read the Bible to see if what they say is true. Know God by reading his Word—not just by what others say about him. (A devotional like this helps, but spend time reading the Bible too.) Choose a book of the Bible to read, and commit to reading it over the next week or weeks. Ask a friend or family member if they will read it at the same time as you. You can even ask each other questions and share your favorite parts.

Write down the book of the Bible you plan to read and who you will read it with. Use this space to keep a log of your Bible reading from day to day.

In the beginning was the Word, and the Word was with God, and the Word was God.

JOHN 1:1

God, help me to read your words in the Bible every day. In Jesus' name, amen.

Wild Wonder

Wood frog eggs hatch fast, sometimes in as few as 9 or 10 days.

Creature Connection

Each frog species makes its own sound. With more than 7,000 species of frogs, that's a lot of sounds. Learn what species of frogs live near you. With an adult's permission, listen to their calls online so you can recognize them.

SEARCH FROGS...

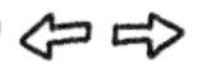

AMERICAN TOAD

WOOD FROG

FOWLER'S TOAD

BULLFROG

In the Wild

In the spring or summer, go outdoors (possibly near a pond or stream) in the evening to listen to frogs. Try to get close enough to see the frogs and confirm their identification.

Eastern Newt

Scientific Name: *Notophthalmus viridescens*

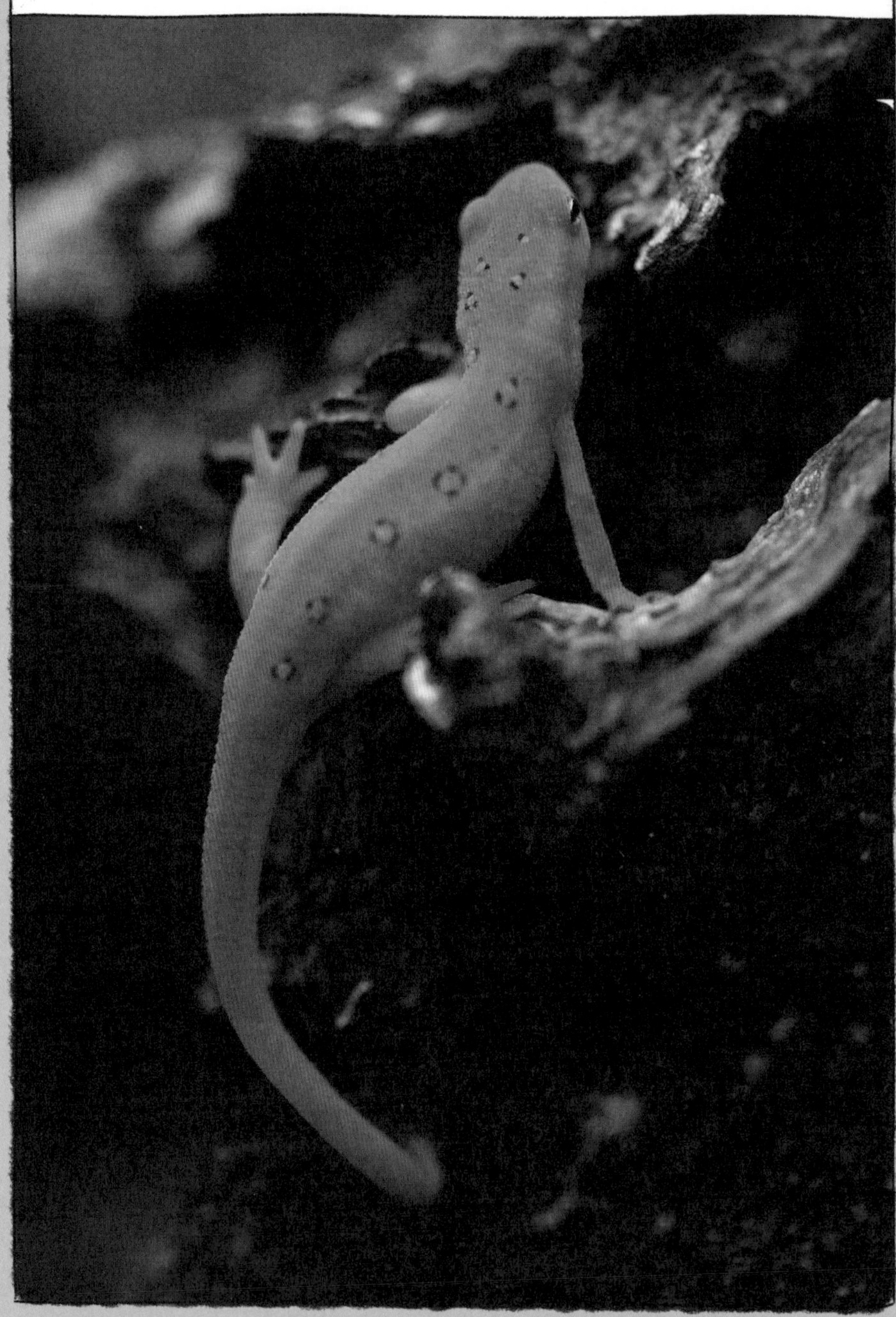

Slow and Steady

Walking along trails in the woods of the midwestern and eastern United States, you might spot a bright-orange salamander with black and red spots. It's so common to see the eastern newt with its young adult coloring that it even has a nickname: the red-spotted newt.

But the eastern newt isn't always orange with red spots. It hatches from the egg as a brownish-green tadpole and breathes through gills. Eventually it develops lungs and transforms into a bright-orange eft (young adult newt stage). After a few years, it becomes a brownish-green adult and lives in the water.

The adult female eastern newt takes her time laying eggs. She deposits just a few eggs each day throughout her breeding habitat. After a couple of weeks, the mother newt finishes laying a total of 200 to 400 jelly-covered eggs attached to underwater grasses. They hatch after a month or two.

It takes a long time to scatter hundreds of eggs throughout the habitat, but the female does this to protect the eggs. Because she spreads the eggs out and takes her time, the eggs are more likely to be safe from predators. When we have a job to do, we can take our time too. Then we'll know the task was done well. It's more important to finish well than to finish quickly. Working to the best of our ability always brings honor to God. Think of a job you sometimes rush. Commit to taking your time to do it well in the future.

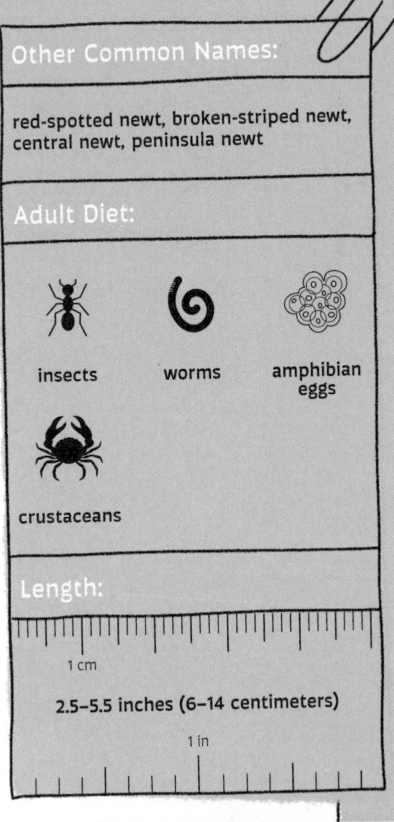

Other Common Names:
red-spotted newt, broken-striped newt, central newt, peninsula newt
Adult Diet:
insects
worms
amphibian eggs
crustaceans
Length:
1 cm
2.5–5.5 inches (6–14 centimeters)
1 in

How do you feel when you know you've done a good job instead of rushing? Write about it here.

Whatever your hand finds to do, do it with your might.

ECCLESIASTES 9:10

Heavenly Father, it feels good to work hard to honor you. Show me if there's a task I can do even better than I have been. In Jesus' name, amen.

Wild Wonder

Eastern newts can live about 15 years in the wild.

Creature Connection

The eastern newt changes color throughout its life. Look at the pictures of the life cycle below. What similarities do you see when the eastern newt is in the tadpole, eft, and adult stages? How are the stages different? Next, look at photographs of yourself when you were a baby, a toddler, a preschooler, and an older kid. What similarities do you see in yourself? How have you changed?

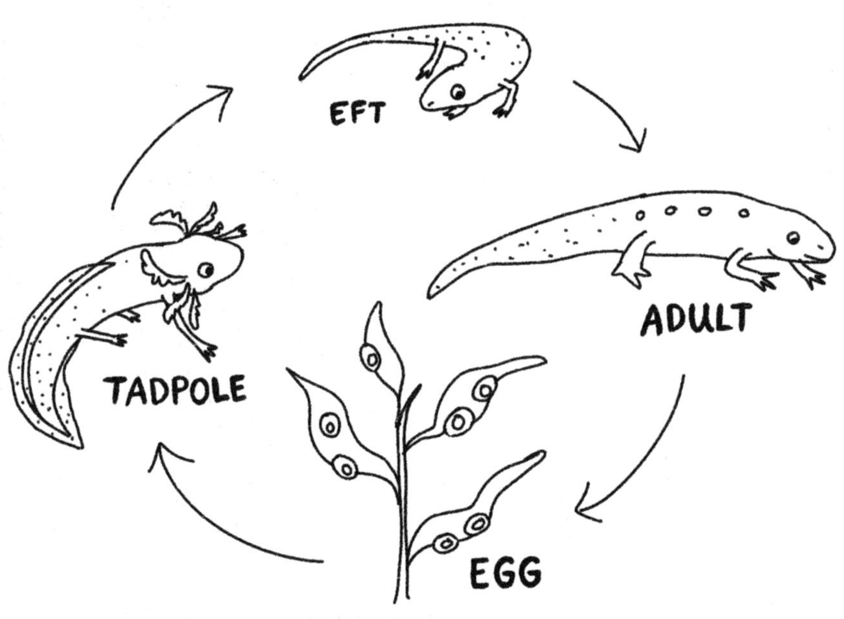

Couch's Spadefoot

Scientific Name: *Scaphiopus couchii*

Soak Up the Rain

All spadefoots get their name from the little nub on each of their hind feet. They use these like the gardening tool called a spade. So it's no surprise spadefoots are expert diggers.

The Couch's spadefoot lives in the southwestern United States and Mexico, where the weather is hot and dry. But it needs water like all amphibians. To stay cool and moist, a Couch's spadefoot chooses a spot in loose, sandy soil. It rocks back and forth and uses its hind feet to shovel out the dirt. Then it goes deep underground to escape the heat of its desert habitat.

The spadefoot leaves its burrow after the annual spring rain to find food and a mate. The male calls for a mate. It sounds like a bleating goat. Later, the female lays up to 3,000 eggs in temporary ponds. Tadpoles hatch in just a day and become froglets in as few as 9 days—before the water dries up.

After just a couple months, the Couch's spadefoot again buries itself underground until the next spring rain. It stays about 3 feet (1 meter) underground for 9 or 10 months a year. Sleeping through the hot, dry weather is called estivation. It's like hibernation but in the summer.

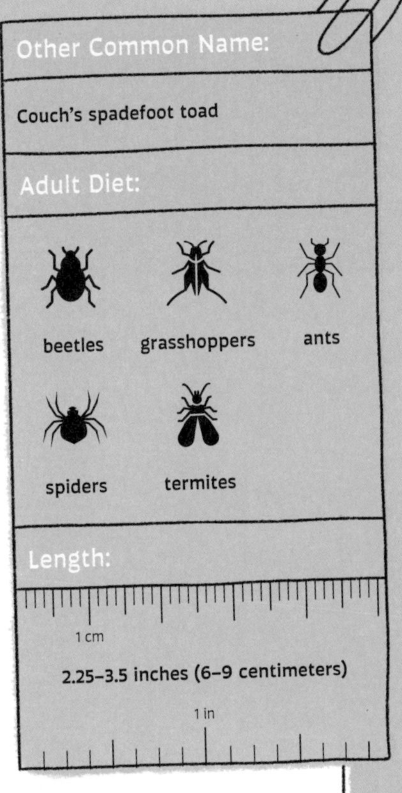

Other Common Name:
Couch's spadefoot toad
Adult Diet:
beetles
grasshoppers
ants
spiders
termites
Length:
1 cm
2.25–3.5 inches (6–9 centimeters)
1 in

God knew this frog would need to dig deep into the soil to survive the dry climate, so he gave the Couch's spadefoot its very own shovel! God knows all about you too. He gives you exactly what you need to get through your tough days so you can persevere in your faith. Rely on God in every way.

How has God provided for you in the past? Write down some specific situations and answers to prayer.

My God will supply every need of yours according to his riches in glory in Christ Jesus.

PHILIPPIANS 4:19

Lord, thank you for giving me everything I need for the challenges in my life. In Jesus' name, amen.

Wild Wonder

One big meal of termites can be enough for a Couch's spadefoot to survive a whole year before eating again.

Creature Connection

Wet two sponges (or washcloths) so they are equally wet. Take them outside. Set one sponge in the sun. Bury the other one in the soil or cover it with a towel. (Or if you want to stay inside, ask an adult for a plastic plate and a container with a lid. Set one sponge on the plate in direct sunlight to dry. Place the other in the lidded container.) After a few hours, compare the two sponges. Which is wetter? A buried frog doesn't dry out quickly either!

Red-Eyed Tree Frog

Scientific Name: *Agalychnis callidryas*

Pop Eyes

As their name suggests, tree frogs spend most of their lives in trees. Red-eyed tree frogs even lay their eggs on vegetation instead of in water. The mama frog lays eggs on—or on the underside of—a leaf overhanging water. A clutch includes about 40 green eggs covered in jelly. The eggs hatch, and—*plop!*—the tadpoles fall into the water. Each one eventually metamorphoses into a slender green frog.

As the red-eyed tree frog rests camouflaged in leaves, it closes a special translucent eyelid called the nictitating membrane. The frog watches through this see-through eyelid for danger. When a predator comes close, the frog surprises the enemy. How? The frog opens its bright-red eyes. Startled, the predator pauses, and the red-eyed tree frog has time to leap to safety.

The red-eyed tree frog may not know exactly which predator is approaching, but it doesn't try to stay and fight. It has an escape plan. Consider a situation when you could be tempted to do something you know is wrong. Think about what options you have to get out of that situation. Then talk to a friend or grown-up and see if they have any more ideas for you. A plan helps, and God always helps too.

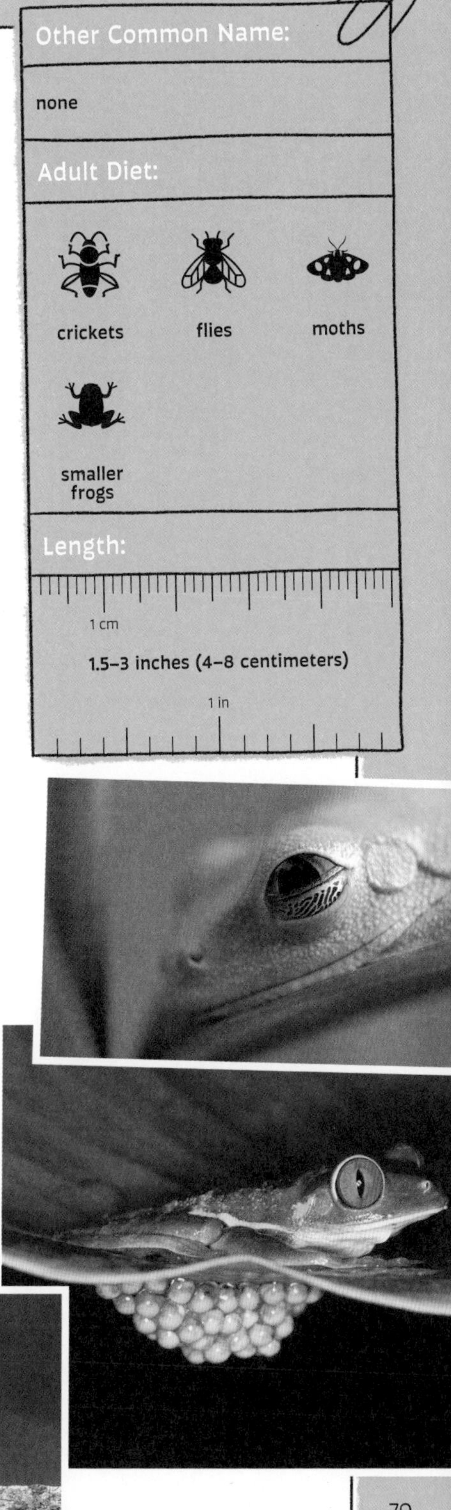

Other Common Name:
none
Adult Diet:
crickets
flies
moths
smaller frogs
Length:
1 cm
1.5–3 inches (4–8 centimeters)
1 in

How can you plan ahead to avoid temptation? Write some thoughts below.

God is faithful, and he will not let you be tempted beyond your ability, but with the temptation he will also provide the way of escape, that you may be able to endure it.

1 CORINTHIANS 10:13

God, thanks for giving me a way out of tough situations and forgiving me when I sin. In Jesus' name, amen.

Wild Wonder

A red-eyed tree frog can lay its eggs as high as 12 feet (3.5 meters) above water.

Creature Connection

The red-eyed tree frog has green skin and red eyes. Look at the color wheel below. Notice how red and green are opposite each other on the wheel. They're called complementary colors. What other color pairs are opposites on the color wheel? Can you think of anything in nature that has complementary colors? Look for examples in a nature book or near your home.

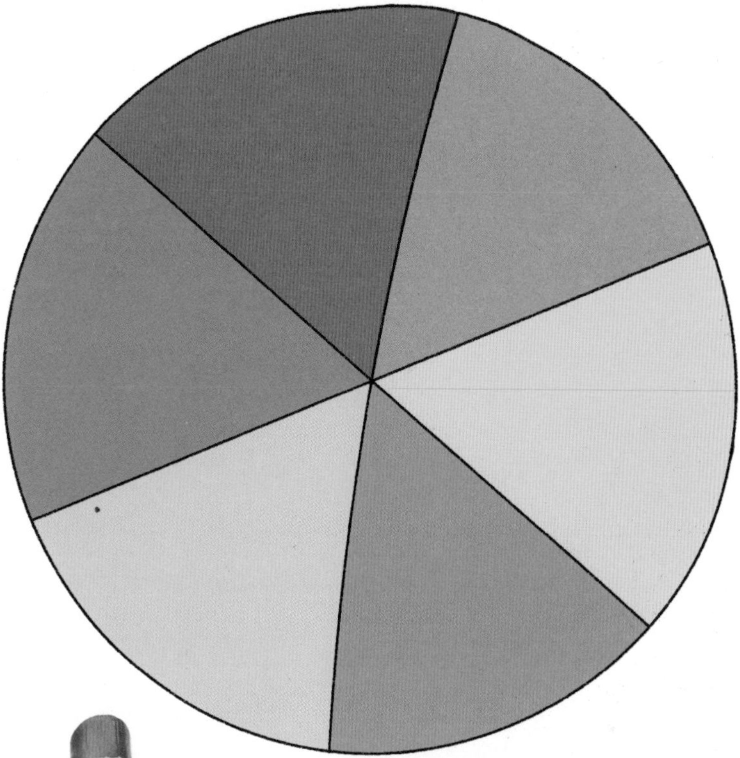

Giant Palm Salamander

Scientific Name: *Bolitoglossa dofleini*

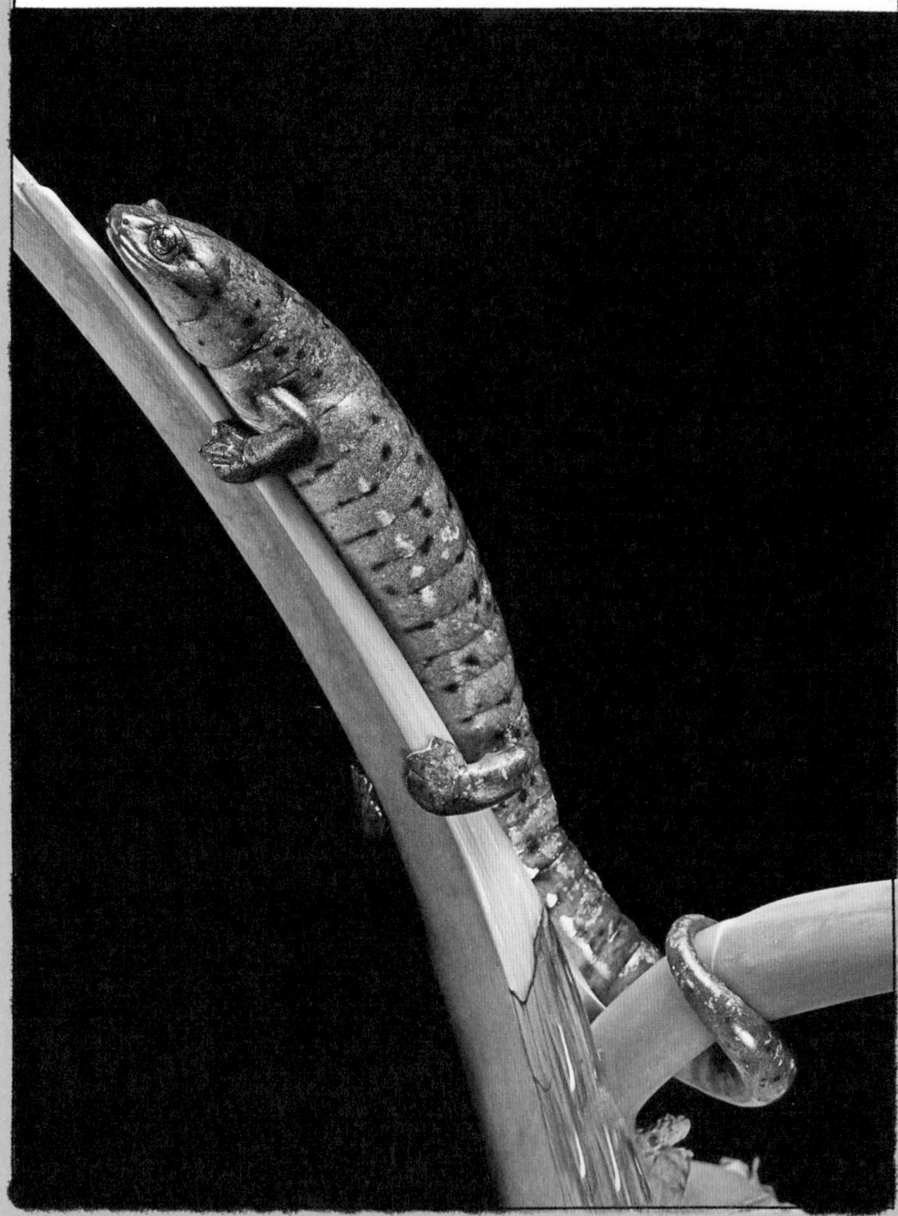

Quick Tongue

Other Common Names:

Alta Verapaz salamander, Doflein's salamander, mushroom-tongued salamander, palm salamander

Adult Diet:

insects spiders

Length:

1 cm

2.75–4.5 inches (7–11.5 centimeters)

1 in

Giant palm salamanders don't grow to giant sizes. But they can fit in the palm of your hand, as the name suggests! Females grow to about 4.5 inches (11.5 centimeters), plus a tail. Males are a bit smaller at 2.75 inches (7 centimeters). But the giant palm salamander takes a long time to grow up. It doesn't reach maturity for at least 10 years. That's slow for amphibians.

Salamanders capture prey with their tongues. The giant palm salamander feasts on invertebrates like spiders and insects. And its tongue is fast. Energy is stored in the rolled-up tongue and released when the tongue launches and snaps up its next meal.

God made nearly 800 kinds of salamanders, and the giant palm salamander has the fastest tongue to capture dinner. Sometimes being fast isn't helpful for people. If we communicate before we think, we often regret it. God doesn't want us to use our tongues with speed. He wants us to think about what we say and not always say the first thing that comes to mind. Be quick to listen to what others are saying, and think carefully about how you should respond—especially when you're feeling upset. Together, these steps help us to be slow to anger.

Ask an adult to help you find some verses about speaking wisely and kindly. Record your favorite one here.

Let every person be quick to hear, slow to speak, slow to anger.

JAMES 1:19

Jesus, help me to think carefully before I speak and to consider how others might be feeling. In your name, amen.

Wild Wonder

It takes the giant palm salamander about 7 milliseconds to pop out its tongue and snatch a meal.

Creature Connection

The giant palm salamander's unrolled tongue has incredible speed and precision. Stretch out the coiled tube of a party horn (also called a party blower). Wet the underside of the tip. Reroll it. Draw a small bug on a piece of paper and then test your accuracy. Blow the horn to try to "capture" the bug. You win when the bug gets wet!

Axolotl

Scientific Name: *Ambystoma mexicanum*

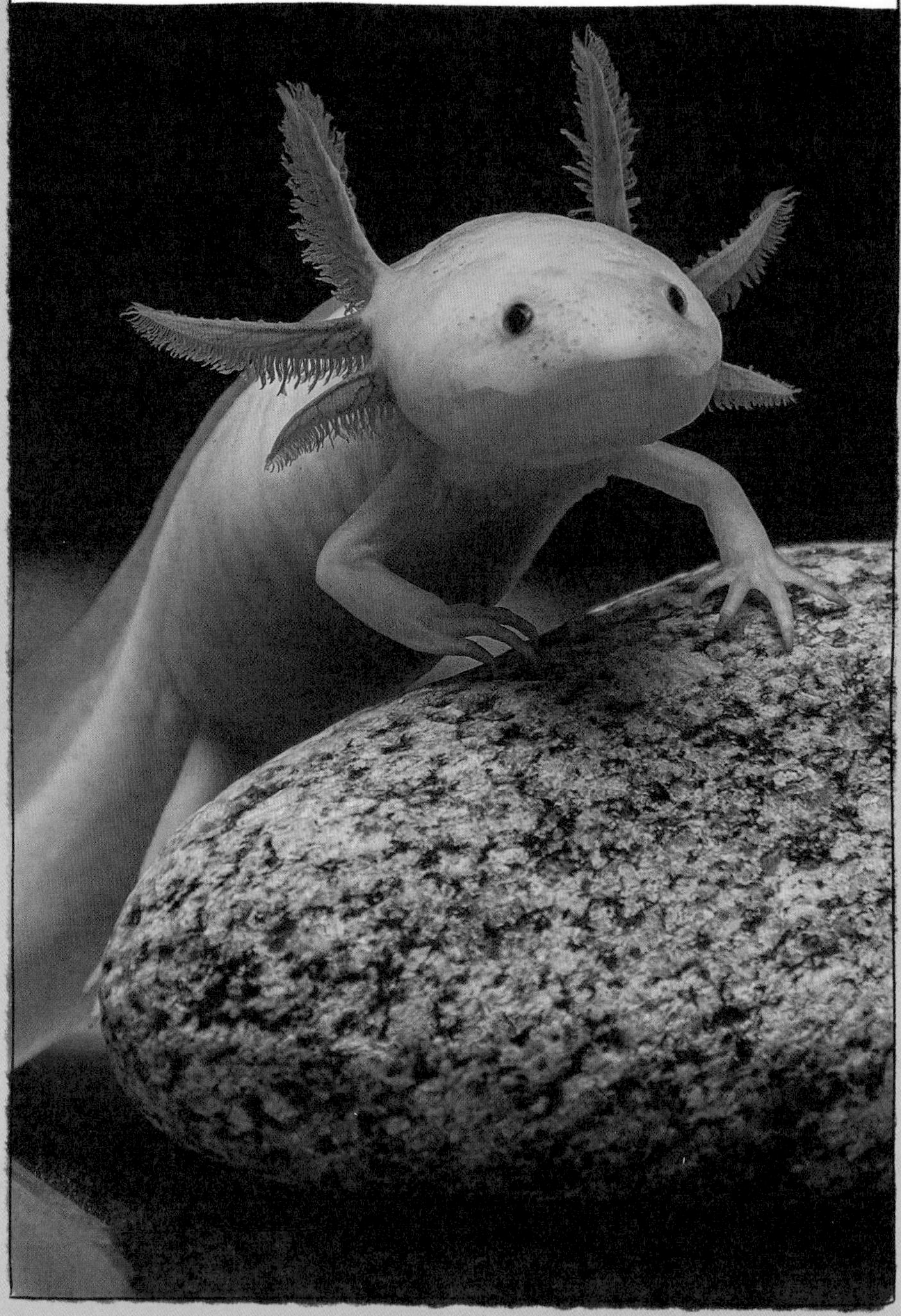

Lookin' Young

The axolotl (pronounced AX-uh-LOT-ul) is an aquatic salamander, found in the wild in only two lakes near Mexico City. Because the water of these lakes is contaminated and the lakes are often drained, the axolotl is nearly extinct in the wild.

Most amphibians have gills when they are young but develop lungs as they grow. But the axolotl is an unusual amphibian. These salamanders—even as adults—look like they never grew up. Those aren't feathers on its head—those are gills!

The mature axolotl may seem like a young salamander at first glance, but it is an adult. It just keeps the characteristic of breathing through gills instead of developing lungs like other adult amphibians.

Other Common Name:

Mexican walking fish

Adult Diet:

insects, worms, fish, salamanders, crustaceans

Length:

1 cm

9–12 inches (23–30 centimeters)

1 in

You're getting older every day, which is a good thing! But even as you grow up, it's good to keep some qualities from childhood, such as faith. Jesus told his followers to receive—to believe in—the Kingdom of God with the faith of a child. All it takes to be a Christian is to believe. (You can still ask questions and even have doubts.)

Read Mark 10:13–16. Why do you think the children loved and trusted Jesus so much? Write down your thoughts.

Truly, I say to you, whoever does not receive the kingdom of God like a child shall not enter it.

MARK 10:15

Heavenly Father, thank you for helping me to believe in you. In Jesus' name, amen.

Wild Wonder

If an axolotl's limb gets hurt or breaks off, it can grow back. Occasionally the axolotl even grows extra limbs.

Creature Connection

Create your own drawing of a cute axolotl. For its head, draw a wide oval. Add eyes that are far apart and a wide mouth. Then include feather-like gills on each side of the head. When you look at your drawing, remember God just wants you to believe with childlike faith.

CUTE!

Glass Frog

Scientific Names: *Chimerella mariaelenae*, *Vitreorana eurygnatha*, *Hyalinobatrachium fleischmanni*, and more

What's Inside?

In the rain forests of Central and South America, glass frogs live in trees. Glass frogs have long limbs and flat, thin bodies. Their sticky toe pads help them cling to slippery leaves and trees—even during the rainy season. Like many frogs, glass frogs are nocturnal, awake at night and asleep during the day.

The skin on a glass frog's chest and belly—the ventral or bottom side—sets it apart from other frogs. The skin is see-through, so light shines through the underside. This gives us an incredible view inside the frog. Like looking through a window, we can see the bones and intestines of a glass frog. We can watch its heart beat and pump blood through its body. The glass frog's translucent skin blends in so well, its legs and toes nearly vanish when the frog sits on a leaf.

The skin of glass frogs gives us a rare look at their anatomy; we see all their inner parts. We have organs like glass frogs, but ours can't be seen by looking through our skin. Amazingly, we also have Jesus inside us through the presence of the Holy Spirit, but others won't know unless we make it obvious. How? Use your words and actions to give others a window to see your faith. Tell your friends about the treasure of Jesus within you.

Other Common Names:
Maria Elena's glass frog, Rio glass frog, Fleischmann's glass frog, and more
Adult Diet:
crickets
moths
flies
spiders
small frogs
Length:
1 cm
0.75–3 inches (2–8 centimeters)
1 in

Do other people know that Jesus lives in you? Write down how you might explain this to a friend. Ask an adult for help if you need to.

I pray that the sharing of your faith may become effective for the full knowledge of every good thing that is in us for the sake of Christ.

PHILEMON 1:6

Jesus, help me to be bold and tell others that I love you. In your name, amen.

Wild Wonder

The bones of glass frogs are often green.

Creature Connection

Have someone trace your body (or your stomach and chest area) on an extra-large piece of newsprint or craft paper (or paper taped together). Research where the heart, lungs, stomach, and other organs are located and draw where they would be on the life-size tracing.

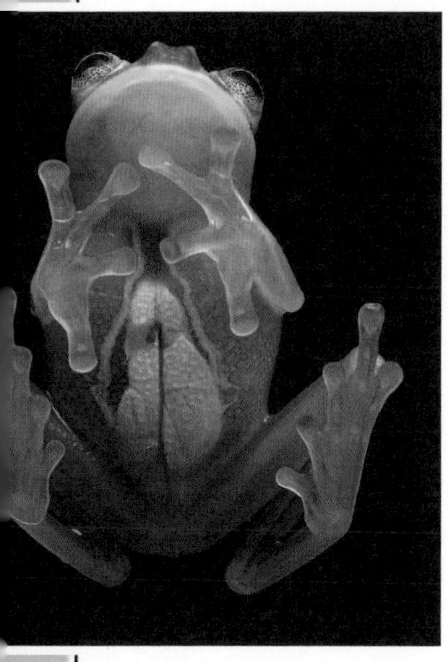

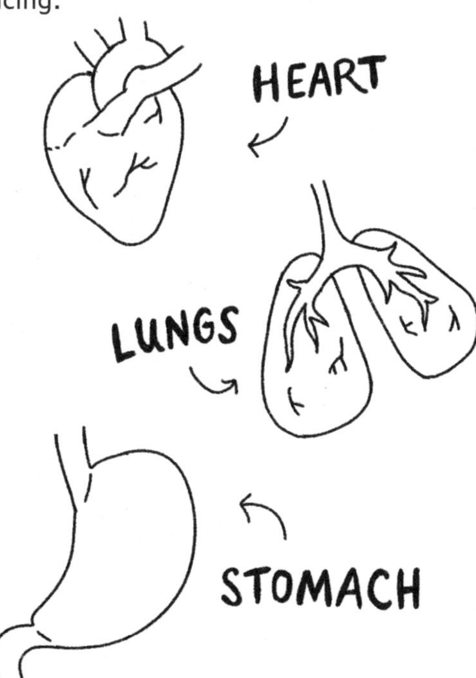

American Bullfrog

Scientific Name: *Lithobates catesbeianus*

Loud and Low

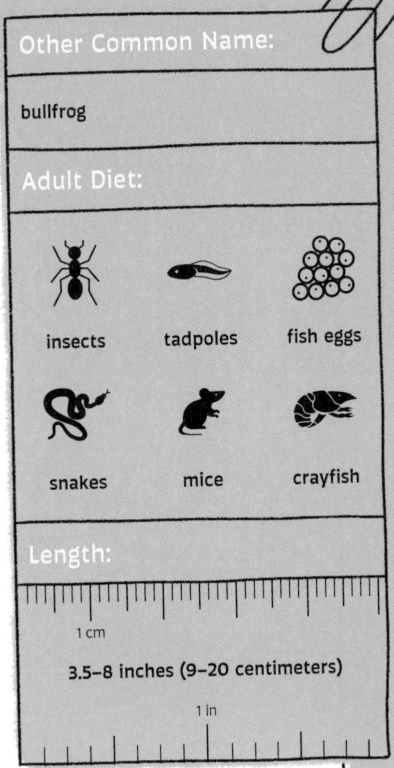

Other Common Name:
bullfrog
Adult Diet:
insects
tadpoles
fish eggs
snakes
mice
crayfish
Length:
1 cm
3.5–8 inches (9–20 centimeters)
1 in

You might spot a big bullfrog in a lake, pond, river, or marsh. American bullfrogs rarely leave the water. When it gets cold, they dig down into the mud and leaf litter to hibernate.

American bullfrogs eat any critter that fits in their mouths. In addition to devouring huge numbers of insects, they've been known to eat rattlesnakes and scorpions. They even gulp down other frogs.

The male bullfrog has a distinctive mating call to advertise to female bullfrogs. It's loud, low, and long—lasting just under a second. The "jug-o-rum" call can be heard more than a half mile (1 kilometer) away.

Bullfrog eggs develop for just 4 days before tadpoles hatch. Bullfrog tadpoles grow to a huge size—longer than an adult's finger. Bullfrogs stay tadpoles for about 3 years. Then they take another couple of years to become mature adults. Adult bullfrogs often weigh more than a pound (half a kilogram).

The deep call of the American bullfrog grabs our attention, but God's call, through the Holy Spirit, isn't always so obvious. He doesn't usually speak aloud to us, but sometimes he reminds us to pray for someone just by prompting us to think about that person. Or we might remember something we had planned to do to encourage someone. When you get little nudges like these from the Holy Spirit, don't wait. Take action right away.

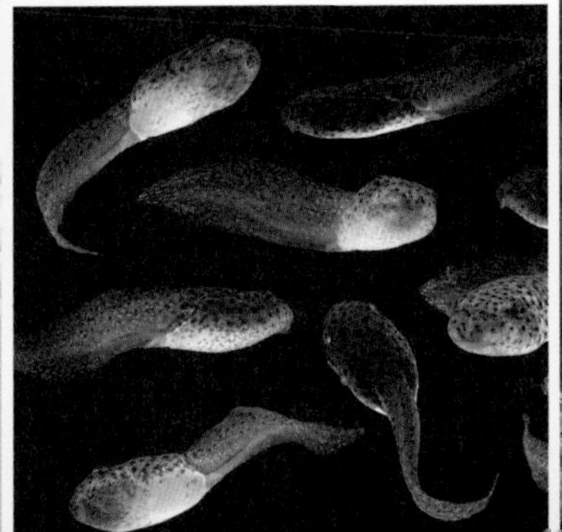

Ask the Holy Spirit to bring to mind some people to pray for or encourage. Then write down your plan for action.

The Helper, the Holy Spirit, whom the Father will send in my name, he will teach you all things and bring to your remembrance all that I have said to you.

JOHN 14:26

God, listening to the sounds of frogs and nature is amazing when we know what to listen for. Help me to listen for your Spirit too. Thank you! In Jesus' name, amen.

Wild Wonder

The female American bullfrog lays as many as 20,000 eggs at a time.

Creature Connection

With an adult's permission, listen to the call of an American bullfrog online. (This site might be helpful: musicofnature.com /calls-of-frogs-and-toads-of-the-northeast.) Compare it to the short and high call of another frog called the spring peeper. They're quite different. Challenge yourself to speak with a long, low tone like the bullfrog. Then try talking more like a spring peeper. Which was more fun?

BULLFROG

SPRING PEEPER

About **10,000** species of birds live around the world and on every continent. (When scientists count subspecies, the numbers nearly double.) Birds hatch from eggs, and most bird parents build nests where their young can grow up safely.

Feathers cover birds' bodies. The feathers keep birds warm and provide coloring, which is useful for camouflage or attracting a mate.

BIRDS

Ruby-Throated Hummingbird

Scientific Name: *Archilochus colubris*

Hmmmmmmm

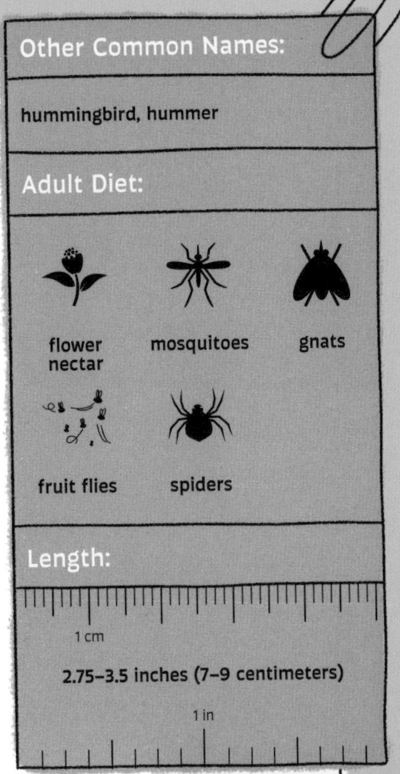

The ruby-throated hummingbird beats its wings about 50 times every second, creating the humming sound you hear as it darts past your ear. These itty-bitty birds weigh only as much as a nickel, but they fly fast, zipping in and out of flowers.

These busy birds live throughout North America and as far south as Costa Rica. They move constantly. Even when they're standing on a perch, they shuffle their feet. But they don't walk or hop.

Hummingbirds perform aerial "tricks," flying backward or upside down. The ruby-throated hummingbird hovers near a flower and then uses its long beak to search for nectar. Its tongue has tubelike grooves that open and fill with nectar. It works like a miniature nectar pump.

When threatened, hummingbirds are aggressive. They peck with their beaks, attack with talons, and beat predators with wings.

Hummingbirds also choose their neighbors carefully to protect their young. They typically build their nests under hawks' nests! You might think that this would be dangerous, but it actually means more hummingbird chicks survive. Hawks are predators, but hummingbirds—and their eggs—are just too small to make a meal for a hawk. Mexican jays do eat hummingbirds, but they don't want to be hunted by the hawk. So the jays don't get too close—and the hummingbird chicks stay safe.

Hawks might not intentionally protect hummingbirds, but God faithfully and intentionally protects you. He knows your past, present, and future. And he guards you against evil. Ask family members to tell you about how God has protected you and your family from harm.

Write down a story of how God protected you or a family member from harm.

The Lord is faithful. He will establish you and guard you against the evil one.

2 THESSALONIANS 3:3

Heavenly Father, thank you for loving me and protecting me. In Jesus' name, amen.

Wild Wonder

Each hummingbird egg is about the size of a pea.

Creature Connection

Hummingbirds can visit over a thousand flowers in a day. You can help feed them by providing a nectar substitute in a hummingbird feeder. Ask an adult for help making the nectar. In a small pan, bring 1 cup (240 milliliters) of boiling water and ¼ cup (60 grams) white sugar to a boil. Stir until dissolved. Allow to cool, then fill a feeder. Hang your feeder outside and wait patiently for hummingbirds to visit.

Brown Kiwi

Scientific Name: *Apteryx australis*, *Apteryx mantelli*, and more

Not the Fuzzy Fruit

Have you ever eaten the fuzzy brown fruit called kiwi (say KEE-wee)? There's also a bird the size of a chicken that lives only in New Zealand called the brown kiwi. At night they call, "Kwee! Kwee! Kwee!" to find mates and protect their territory.

Brown kiwis prefer to live in the darkness of large forests. Rather shy, brown kiwis hide in their burrows until night when they search for food. They use their long bills to dig in the dirt and smell for worms and insects. Since their nostrils are at the end of their bills, sometimes dirt gets stuck. To get the dirt out, they blow and snort.

Looking at a brown kiwi, you might think it's not very birdlike. Its feathers look and feel like fur. It uses its sense of smell like a lot of mammals do. The brown kiwi has whiskers made from feathers that it uses to sense and feel its environment. The kiwi's wings are so tiny, they are hard to see and useless for flying. Unlike most birds, the brown kiwi has heavy bones; it cannot fly.

Kiwis are the national symbol of New Zealand and a source of pride for the people there. These birds are displayed on money, road signs, and sports uniforms. The kiwi population is vulnerable, and conservation efforts are helping them to not become endangered or extinct. Starting with Adam and Eve, God gave all of us authority over animals, which includes the responsibility to care for them. What can you do today to show respect for God by caring for his creation?

What plants and animals live in your yard or neighborhood? List some ways you can care for them.

Have dominion over the fish of the sea and over the birds of the heavens and over every living thing that moves on the earth.

GENESIS 1:28

Dear God, help me to care for this incredible world you made. In Jesus' name, amen.

Wild Wonder

If kiwi chicks survive their first year of life, they typically live about 20 years in the wild.

Creature Connection

Build your own brown kiwi bird for a snack. You will need one kiwi fruit, a grape, a raisin, and 3 almonds. (You can also substitute other foods to build your kiwi.) Cut the kiwi in half and lay one half of it green side down on a plate. Set aside the other half. Cut the grape in half and use one half as the bird's head. From the other half of the grape, cut out a shape of a tiny wing and place it on the bird's side. Use the almonds as a beak and legs and add a raisin to create an eye.

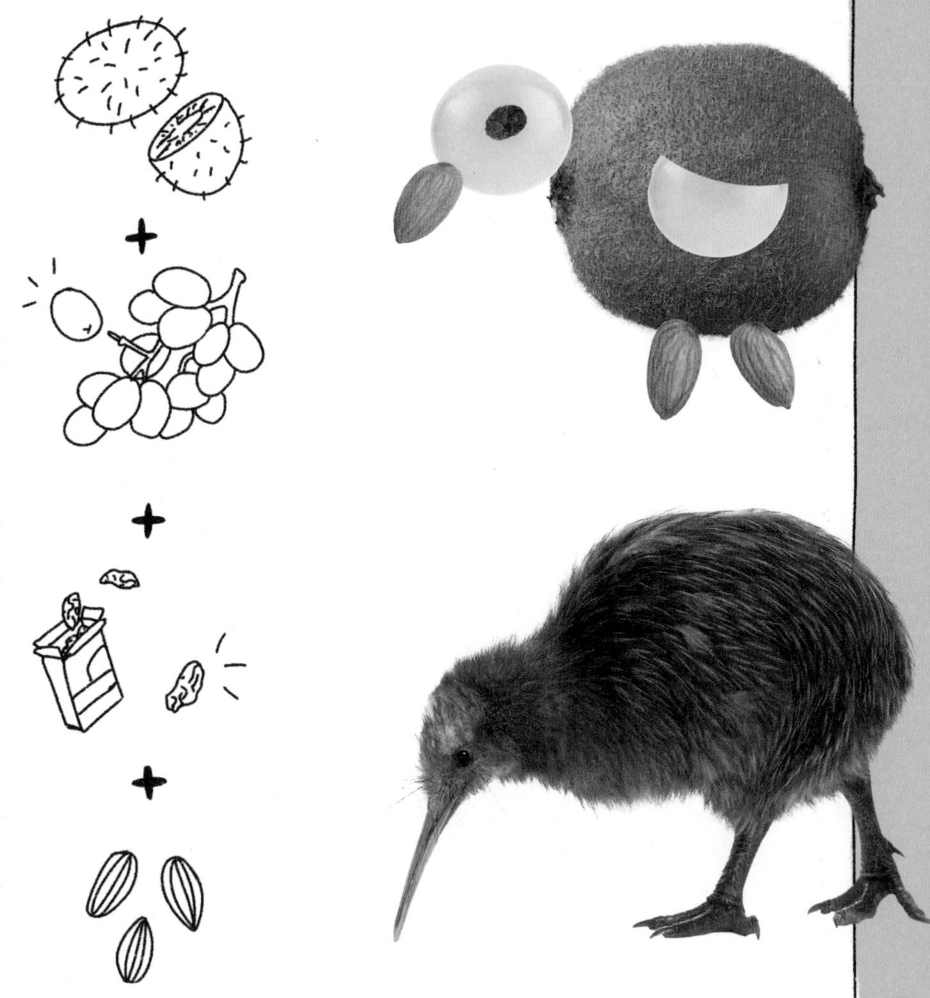

Common Loon

Scientific Name: *Gavia immer*

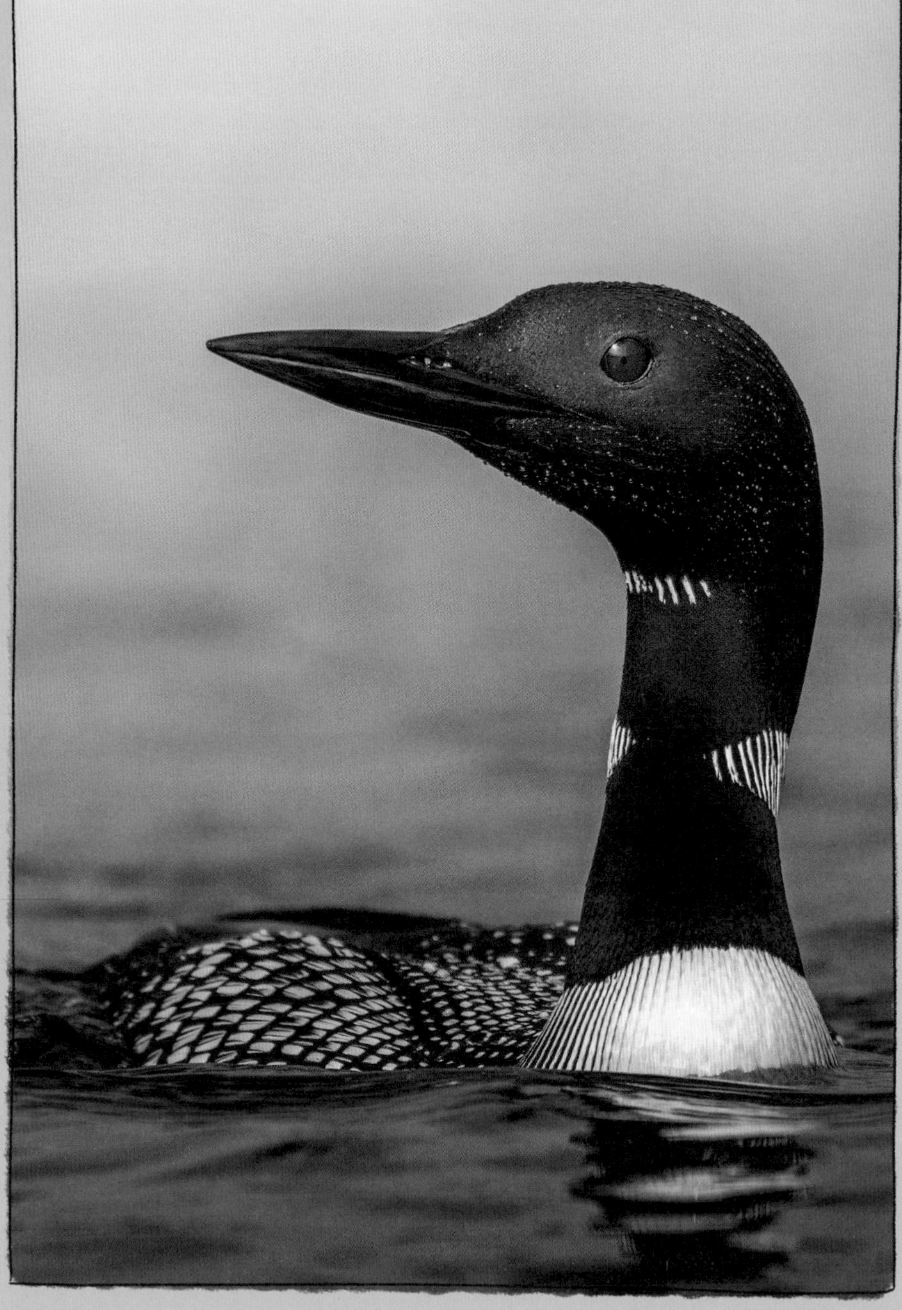

Water Runners

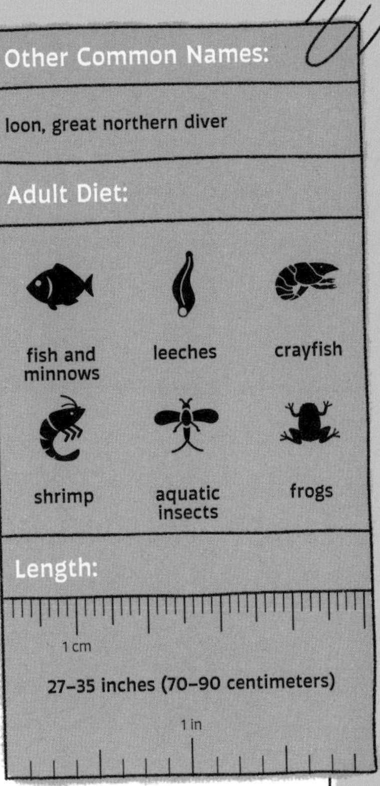

Common loons primarily live in North America. They make their homes on lakes and large ponds, where they feast on fish, crayfish, shrimp, and more. And these waterbirds eat a lot! A pair of loons and their 2 chicks can eat about 1,500 pounds (680 kilograms) of fish in a season.

Loons go to shore to mate and lay eggs, but because their legs are set far back on their bodies, it's hard and awkward for them to walk on land. Yet this design is best for loons since it propels them underwater. They swim beneath the surface, using their red eyes to hunt for fish and other water creatures by sight.

Loons fly up to 70 miles (113 kilometers) per hour when migrating to the Gulf of Mexico. Like an airplane, loons need a "runway" to take off to fly. They flap their wings and run across the top of the water to gain speed for liftoff. But if they mistakenly land on a pond that is too small or on a wet road, they can become stranded.

Common loons can walk on land when they need to, but as waterbirds, they excel at swimming and diving in the water—even running on top of the water. God makes each of us unique. You might be great at chess but not baseball. You might be able to sing a beautiful song but can't remember how to multiply fractions. Keep doing what you're great at, and don't be afraid to do activities that are hard. Remember, your value comes from God. He thinks you are precious just as you are.

Ask God to show you if there are any skills you should focus on improving or new activities he wants you to be brave to try. Write your plans here.

You are precious in my eyes, and honored, and I love you.

ISAIAH 43:4

Lord, thank you for helping me to enjoy things I'm good at and persist at hard things too. In Jesus' name, amen.

Wild Wonder

The mournful wail of a common loon lets other loons know where to find it.

Creature Connection

Loons' legs are set far back on their bodies, which is great for diving and swimming, but makes walking on land difficult. Try walking like a loon. Squat down and hold your ankles with your hands. Then walk!

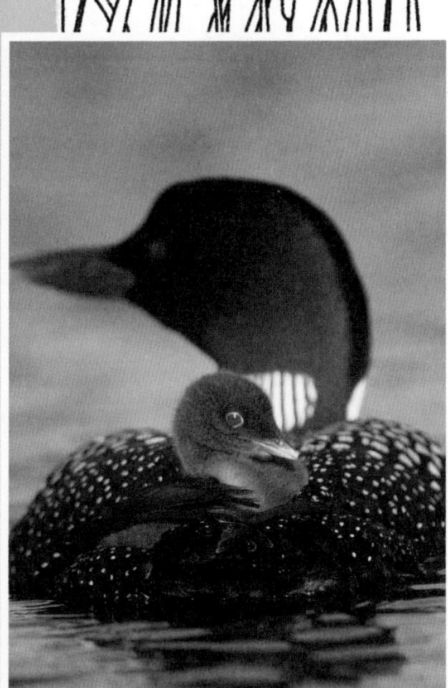

Hoatzin

Scientific Name: *Opisthocomus hoazin*

What's the Stink?

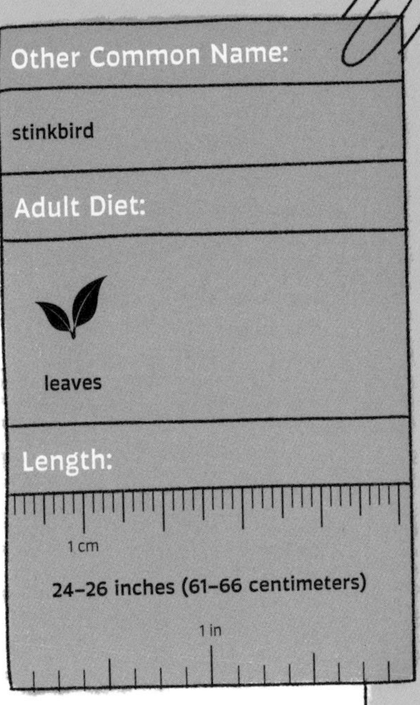

Other Common Name:
stinkbird
Adult Diet:
leaves
Length:
1 cm
24–26 inches (61–66 centimeters)
1 in

The hoatzin (say wat-SEEN) looks a bit like a puppet or even a wild chicken. This blue-faced bird with a rust-colored crest and long tail lives on the banks of the Amazon River and other swamps, rivers, and lakes in South America.

The hoatzin builds its nest on branches that overhang water. Hoatzin chicks can't fly until nearly 3 months of age, but they can swim. If a predator like a snake or monkey comes along, a baby hoatzin escapes with a belly flop to the water below. When danger passes, it swims to land and climbs up the tree.

How does it climb? The young hoatzin has clawed wings. The claws help it to grip as it scales the tree and returns to the nest. Grown hoatzin do not have clawed wings.

The hoatzin is a special kind of herbivore called a folivore. That means it mostly eats leaves from plants. But leaves are hard to digest, so hoatzin have multiple "stomachs" like a cow. Stomach bacteria help to break down leaves through fermentation. This whole process produces methane gas, which stinks. Not surprisingly, the hoatzin's burps have given it the nickname of "stinkbird."

Hoatzin know they need to fuel their bodies with leaves even if it makes a foul smell. Sometimes people can be rude and unkind to Christians—acting as if Christians stink. Jesus said God blesses us when people insult us because of our faith. It can be hard, but we have the responsibility to love others even if this happens. Be kind, even when others aren't.

Has anyone ever been rude to you because of your faith? Make some notes on how you can respond kindly when that happens.

> Blessed are you when people insult you, persecute you and falsely say all kinds of evil against you because of me.
>
> **MATTHEW 5:11, NIV**

Father, thank you for blessing me even when others treat me poorly. Help me to show your love to them. In Jesus' name, amen.

Wild Wonder

Hoatzins are the only bird in the world that eats only leaves.

Creature Connection

Some say the hoatzin reminds them of a chicken combined with a peacock. Invent your own bird. Ask an adult if you can use the Internet to look at a variety of birds from all over the world for inspiration. Choose the shape and size for the head and body. Will it have long or short feathers? What kind of feet and beak? Will it have any additional special features? Now draw and name your bird.

Turkey Vulture

Scientific Name: *Cathartes aura*

Feasting on Decay

Other Common Name:

turkey buzzard

Adult Diet:

carrion (dead animals)

animal waste

Length:

1 cm

25–32 inches (64–81 centimeters)

1 in

Have you ever spotted large brown birds with bald red heads feasting on a carcass along a highway? If so, you've probably spotted a turkey vulture.

These birds with a 6-foot wingspan feed on dead animals. If the turkey vultures live near farms or ranches, they'll likely feast on the dead bodies of livestock. In other areas, they rely on roadkill to survive. Turkey vultures have a keen sense of smell. They actually locate carcasses by odor as well as by sight.

Research shows that the bald skin on vultures' heads and necks helps them stay the right temperature. In hot weather, they can stretch their necks and expose more of their skin to cool off. They can keep more heat in their bodies when soaring at chilly high altitudes by hunching their necks.

Turkey vultures are surprisingly important to the ecosystem. As scavengers, they play a vital cleanup role by eating dead animal carcasses and even poop. Your church is like an ecosystem where everyone has a role to play too. Volunteers help to teach and lead worship. Others set up or clean up. Some may plant flowers or tidy toys. Even greeting a stranger or showing a newcomer where to go is important. Think about how you can help and serve at your church. Ask a staff member or your family if they have any ideas for you.

List some ways you could help at your church, officially or unofficially.

Each of us has one body with many parts. And the parts do not all have the same purpose. So also we are many persons. But in Christ we are one body. And each part of the body belongs to all the other parts.

ROMANS 12:4-5, NIRV

Dear Jesus, thank you for using me to help others at church. In your name, amen.

Wild Wonder

If a predator gets too close, a turkey vulture vomits a partially digested meal, which stinks and makes the predator leave.

Creature Connection

Watch smaller scavengers help decompose a piece of fruit. Place a cut piece of fruit outside (and away from the road). It could be in a garden or by a fence. Each day for a week, look at how the fruit changes. Watch for animal visitors. Record your observations in a notebook. Include drawings of the fruit and note any visible changes as well as visitors you may have seen. Be sure to date and label each drawing. (If you don't have a yard, consider putting the fruit on a paper plate on your porch.)

European Starling

Scientific Name: *Sturnus vulgaris*

Sky Dancer

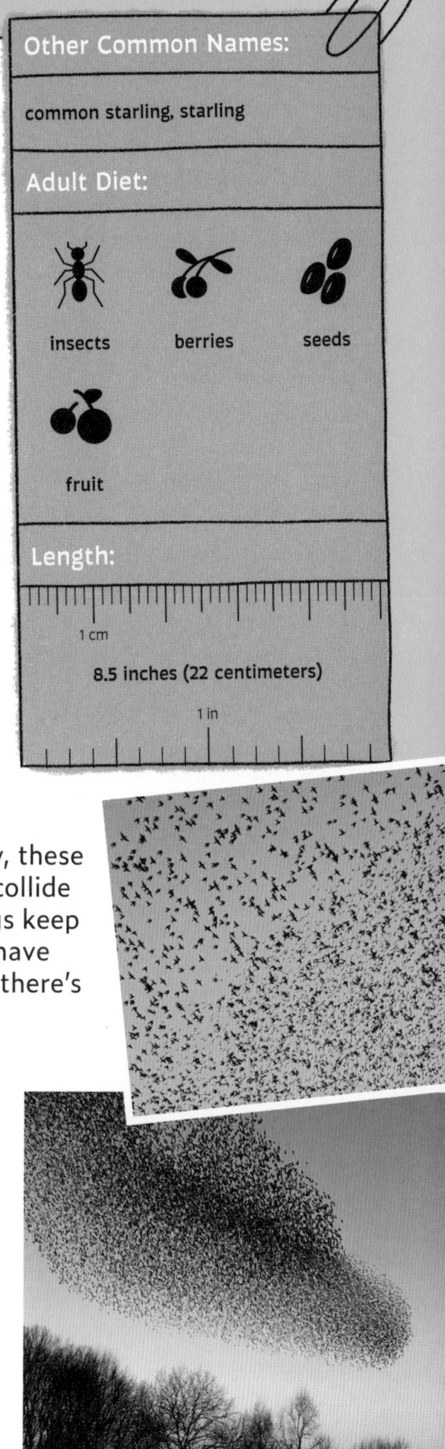

The European starling first came to North America in the early 1890s when 100 starlings were set free in New York City. These birds eat a variety of foods and thrive in diverse habitats. They live in cities and open fields as well as parks and farms. Because of their ability to adapt and their aggressive behavior, European starlings have become abundant across the continent.

Starlings are songbirds. Their songs include warbles and gurgles, chatters and chirrups, and whistles and clicks. They also mimic other animals like frogs, jays, and cats.

Giant groups of European starlings dance together. Each flock's sky dance, called a murmuration, might last for a few minutes or nearly an hour. Amazingly, these groups of flying and dancing birds never collide with one another. Scientists think starlings keep space between themselves because they have quick reactions and incredible vision. But there's more.

In the giant groups, starlings don't watch what every bird in the group does. Instead, each starling watches just 6 or 7 of the other starlings closest to it. Just as European starlings watch out for their closest neighbors, you can do the same. This world has more than 8 billion people in it. Though you might want to help everyone, you probably cannot—but you could start by caring for a few at a time. Talk to someone about how you might help others. Jesus tells us to love our neighbor. Caring for others—even strangers—is one way to show love.

How have you seen people around you care for each other? Could you do some of these things on your own? Could you do some of them with the help of an adult? Make a list of some ideas.

You shall love the Lord your God with all your heart and with all your soul and with all your strength and with all your mind, and your neighbor as yourself.

LUKE 10:27

God, thank you for the people in my community. Help me to love and care for them. In Jesus' name, amen.

Wild Wonder

Murmuration groups can be as small as 500 or as large as 5 million starlings.

Creature Connection

After watching a video of a murmuration, dance together with a few friends or family. Without a prior plan, dance and move around the room so you are close but not touching one another. See if you can dance and move for more than a minute without colliding.

Burrowing Owl

Scientific Name: *Athene cunicularia*

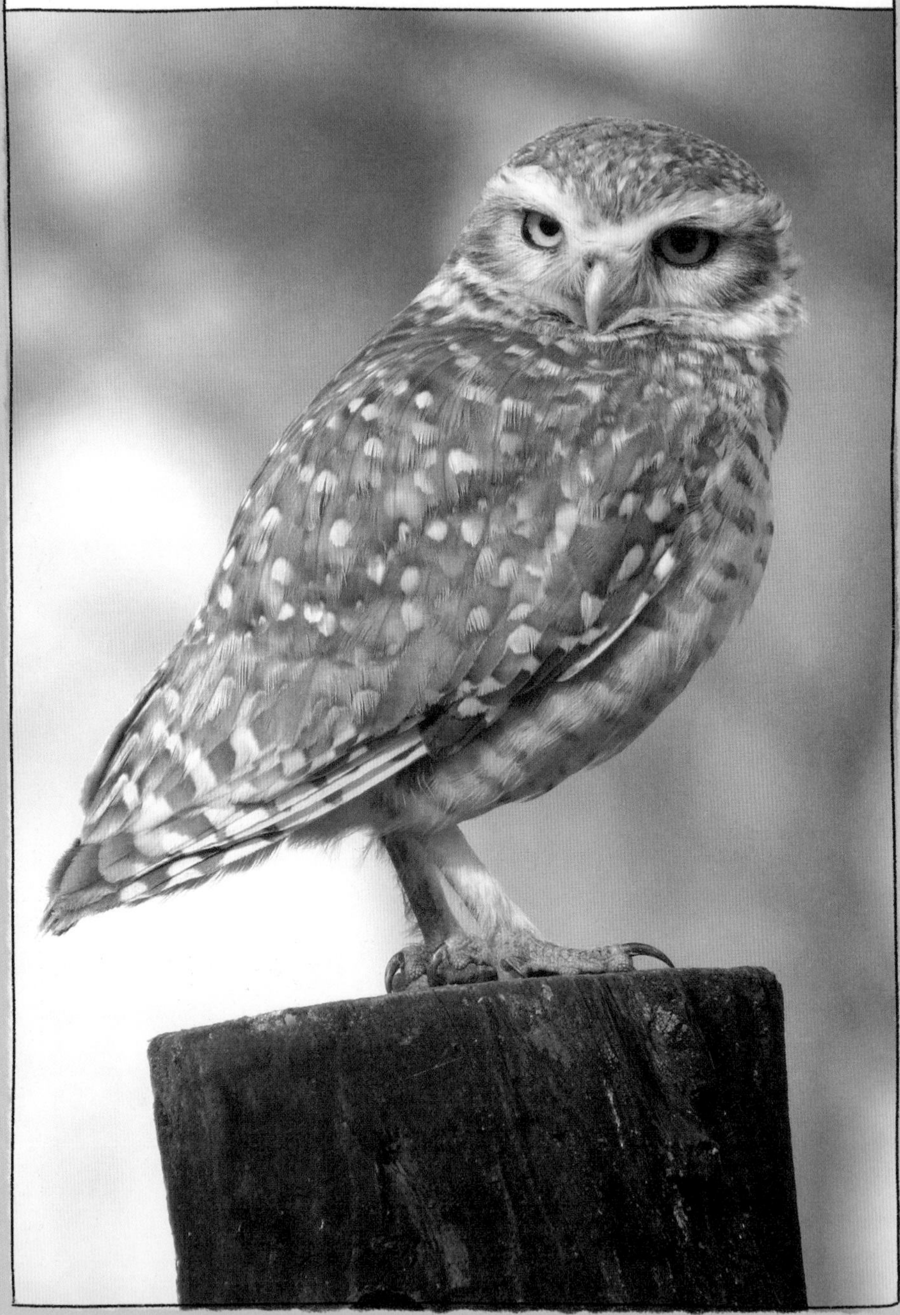

Daytime Hunter

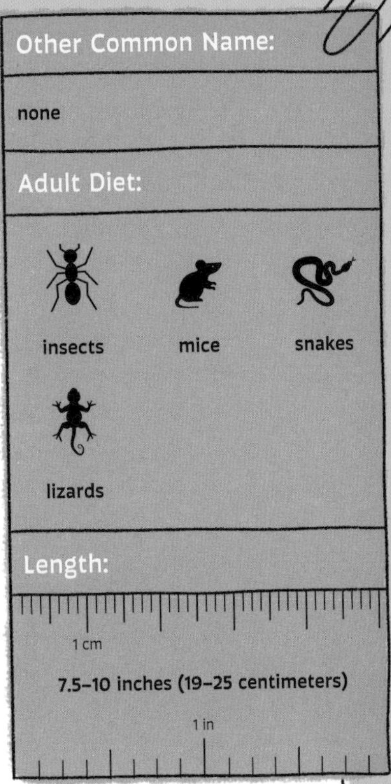

Standing 9 inches tall, the burrowing owl weighs only as much as an apple. These brown owls have bright yellow eyes with white eyebrows and what looks like a white chin strap. With no ear tufts and long legs, these owls stand out from the rest.

Burrowing owls live in deserts, plains, prairies, and fields. Some form colonies with several pairs nesting in the same area. Their underground nests are typically other animals' abandoned burrows, like the prairie dog, gopher, or coyote. But some burrowing owls, especially in Florida, dig their own burrows. Sunlight doesn't reach the bottom of the burrow since they're angled downward and about 10 feet (3 meters) long.

At the bottom of the burrow, males line the nest with grass and roots. They also add a pungent substance to the entrance and nest chamber to keep predators away: cow manure. The parent owls want to keep their round, white eggs safe so the owlets can hatch.

Unlike most owls, burrowing owls are diurnal, which means they're active throughout the day. They hunt mostly around sunrise and sunset. They look for meals—often insects—from both the ground and the air.

God gave owls a keen sense of hearing so they can hunt for food. In this way, he provides what they need. He knows exactly what you need too—food, clothing, and somewhere to live. He doesn't want you to worry. Instead, he wants you to trust that as your heavenly Father, he will take care of you. Trust him today.

Write a prayer asking God to provide for you or someone you know who has a need. Pray the prayer regularly while you wait to see how God will answer.

Look at the birds of the air: they neither sow nor reap nor gather into barn and yet your heavenly Fathe feeds them. Are you not of more value than they?

MATTHEW 6:26

Lord, thank you for giving me food, clothing, and other things I need. In Jesus' name, amen.

Wild Wonder

Burrowing owls take dust baths by flicking dust and dirt on themselves to get rid of mites.

Creature Connection

Like all owls, burrowing owls have exceptional hearing. The feathers around their eyes and ears funnel sounds into their ears. You can hear better than normal by creating "owl ears." Keeping your fingers together, create cups with your hands. Place your cupped hands behind your ears (not over). This makes your ears "bigger" and funnels more sounds into them. Listen for a few minutes to outdoor sounds.

More than **30,000** species of fish live around the world. About half swim in freshwater rivers and lakes. The other half live in saltwater oceans.

Fish breathe through gills, and most hatch from eggs. When water enters the mouth of a fish, it passes through the gills. These gills absorb oxygen from the water. The oxygen moves to the blood, and the heart pumps the blood throughout the body, carrying the oxygen to the organs.

FISH

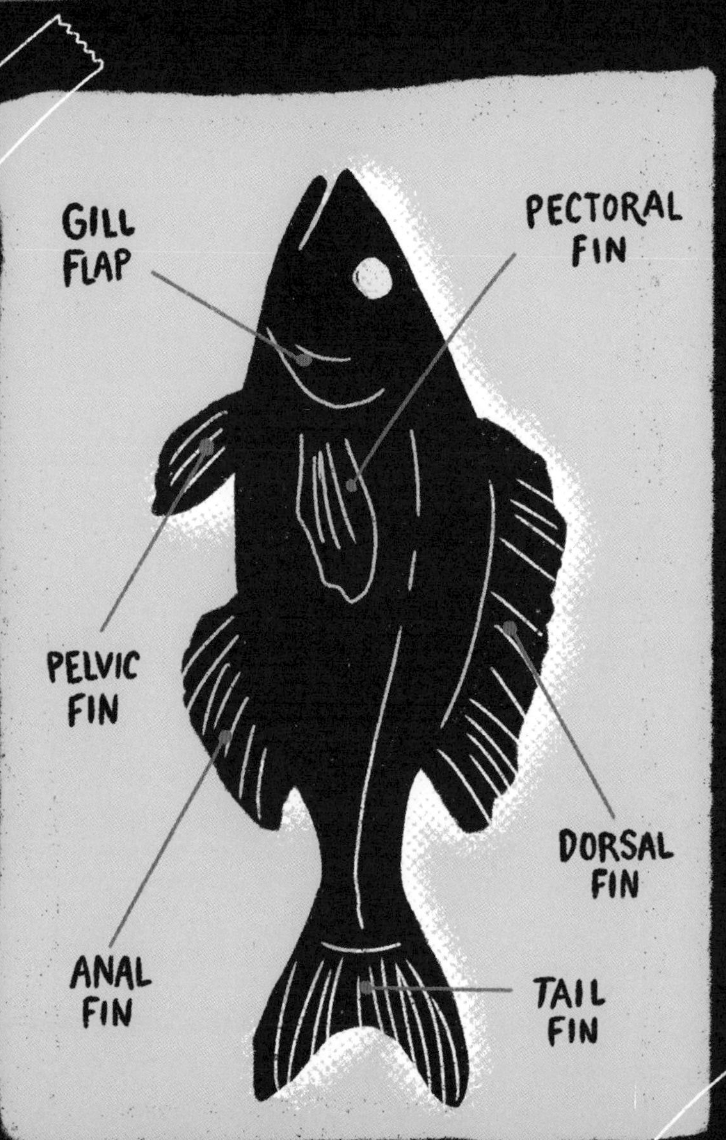
GILL FLAP
PECTORAL FIN
PELVIC FIN
DORSAL FIN
ANAL FIN
TAIL FIN

Stonefish

Scientific Name: *Synanceia verrucosa*

Masters of Camouflage

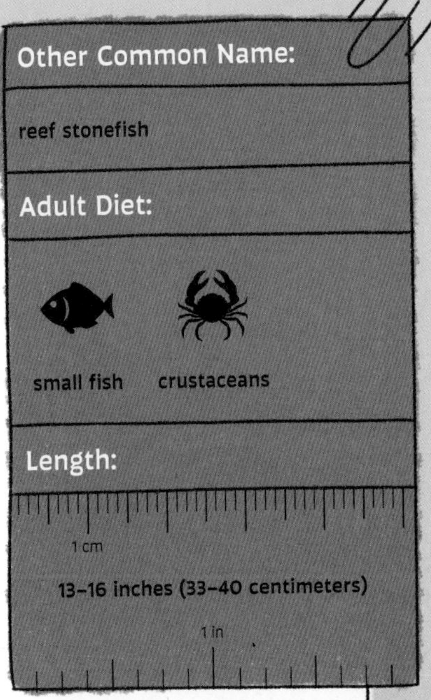

Stonefish live alone as bottom dwellers on the ocean floor. They move very little. Stonefish hop along the sand instead of swimming like other fish. They use their fins to burrow deep into mud or sand when hunting prey. The bumps covering their stocky bodies help them blend in. Their colors change to match their habitat of coral and rocks, making them masters of camouflage.

When hunting, the stonefish waits for dinner to come near. It might wait for hours. Then, when a shrimp gets close, the stonefish sucks its dinner into its huge mouth.

The stonefish's large dorsal fins are usually bent over. This hides 12 to 14 grooved spines that are sharp enough to pierce divers' shoes. At the base of each grooved spine is a large sac of venom.

The stonefish, the deadliest of all fish, only uses its venom sting as a defense when in danger. If a human touches or steps on a stonefish, the sting is painful and can be fatal, but a special medication saves the person's life if given soon enough. Sin in our lives creates pain too. Though it's not always physical pain, we do face problems and heartache because of sin. No matter what we have done, we can ask God to forgive us for our sins. And he does—God forgives us when we ask!

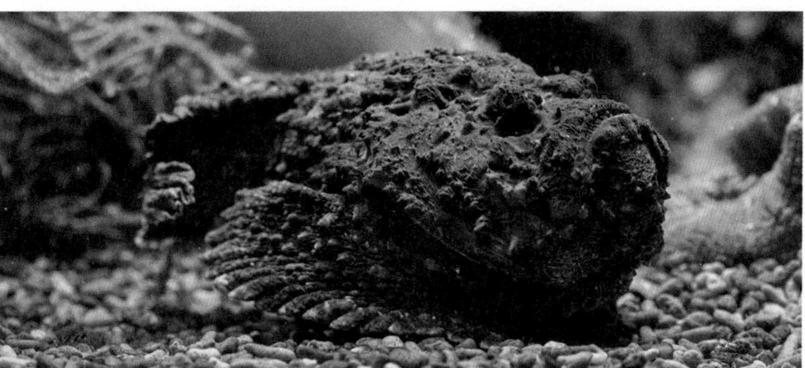

Think of one or more specific ways you have sinned this week. Ask God to forgive you, then jot down a plan to make things right with anyone you sinned against.

> My little children, I am writing these things to you so that you may not sin. But if anyone does sin, we have an advocate with the Father, Jesus Christ the righteous.
>
> **1 JOHN 2:1**

Jesus, thank you for saving me from the poison of sin. In your name, amen.

Wild Wonder
Stonefish move so little, algae sometimes cover their bodies.

Creature Connection

Research venomous and poisonous animals in your region. Consult field guides or search online with an adult's permission. For example, you might search "venomous reptiles in Pennsylvania" and learn there are 21 snake species found in Pennsylvania, and that the 3 venomous snakes in Pennsylvania all try to avoid humans. Create a list or draw each animal in its natural habitat, such as a stream, forest, or meadow. Note if there is anything special about each one.

Poison or Venom?

Poison and venom mean similar things, but they are transferred in different ways. Poison is touched, eaten, or drunk. Animal venom is always injected.

If a person has been exposed to poison or venom, they may need medical help. If the victim cannot be awakened, collapses, has trouble breathing, or has a seizure, call 911 immediately. If you have a nonemergency concern involving venom or poison (including medications, household cleaners, plants, and animals), call the Poison Control Center at 1-800-222-1222.

Whale Shark

Scientific Name: *Rhincodon typus*

The Largest Fish

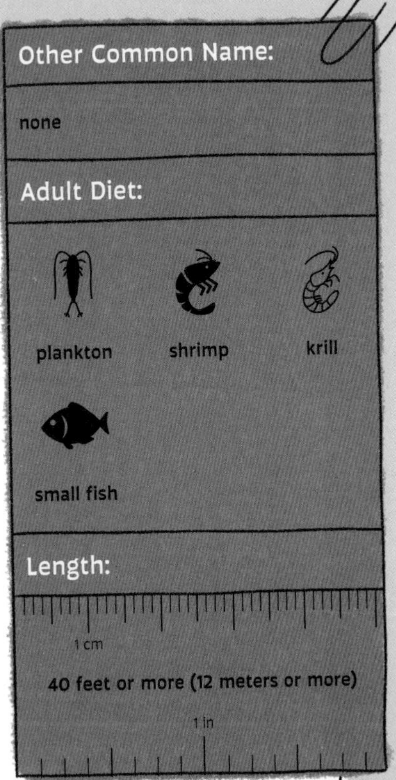

At about 40 feet (12 meters) in length, the massive whale shark is as long as a school bus. This creature may be as large as a whale—but it's not a whale (despite its name). It's a shark. And it's the biggest fish in the sea.

This giant fish's mouth spans 4 or 5 feet (1 or 1.5 meters) in width. (That's as tall as the author of this book.) Inside the mouth, thousands of tiny teeth grow. But the whale shark doesn't bite or chew. Instead it filter-feeds. This means the whale shark swims with its mouth wide open, allowing water and small creatures to enter. It filters about 1,500 gallons (5,678 liters) of water every hour through its gills and then swallows the plankton, krill, and tiny fish it collects. Whale sharks feed at the surface of the ocean, but they can dive down more than a half mile (over 800 meters).

Whale sharks swim slowly—about 2 to 3 miles (3 to 5 kilometers) per hour. They typically swim alone, but in the summer, they migrate thousands of miles with other whale sharks to warm waters rich in plankton, where they feed and mate. But the whale shark doesn't lay her eggs like other fish. The eggs develop inside her. Later, when the female whale shark is alone, she gives birth to live pups.

Whale sharks are an endangered species. Few survive to adulthood. But those that do may live more than 100 years. Though people can live a long time (sometimes as long as whale sharks!), we don't know what will happen to us and our loved ones. Only God knows what our future holds. Each day is a new opportunity. What can you do today to use the time God has given you to love him and others?

Would you make different choices if you knew how long your life was going to be? Make a list of important opportunities and another of nice-but-not-necessary activities.

Be very careful, then, how you live—not as unwise but as wise, making the most of every opportunity.

EPHESIANS 5:15-16, NIV

Father God, thank you for this day. Help me use today to show kindness to others and grow closer to you. In Jesus' name, amen.

Wild Wonder

Whale sharks have tiny teeth on their eyeballs to protect their vision.

Creature Connection

Does it surprise you to learn that not all sharks are looking to chomp big meals? Sharks are often misunderstood. Learn more about sharks at a site such as usa.oceana.org/shark-myths-vs-facts (check with an adult first) or read the author's book *Chomp! The Truth About Sharks* (Reycraft Books). While researching, enjoy mini marshmallows to remind yourself of the shape of whale shark teeth or a sandwich cut into pointy triangles to think of the teeth of a great white shark.

Fathead Minnow

Scientific Name: *Pimephales promelas*

Male Fathead Minnow

Female Fathead Minnow

Smelly Distraction

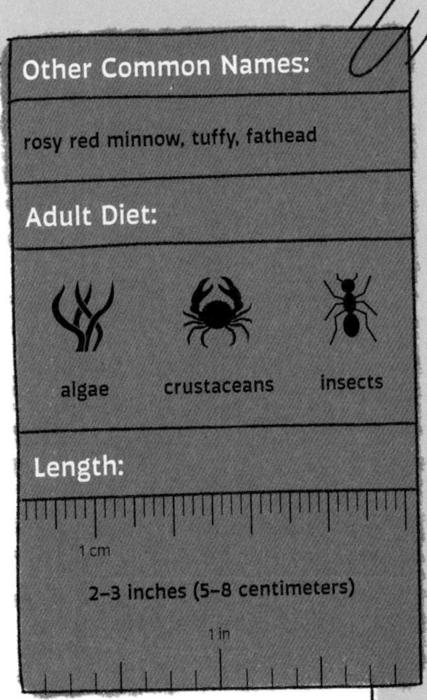

Other Common Names:
rosy red minnow, tuffy, fathead
Adult Diet:
algae
crustaceans
insects
Length:
1 cm
2–3 inches (5–8 centimeters)
1 in

Fathead minnows live in most North American creeks and ponds. But they're easy to miss. Their greenish bodies and clear fins help them camouflage. These small fish easily adapt to different habitats and conditions, making them common in ponds as well as muddy streams.

Male fathead minnows prepare a nest for eggs under a rock or log. Then the female lays about 400 tiny eggs, 1 to 2 millimeters in size. A female fathead minnow lays up to 10,000 eggs in one season. The eggs hatch after about 4 to 5 days, and the baby fish are called fry.

Within a day or two of hatching, fathead minnows sift through mud looking for their next meal. These fish feast on algae, crustaceans, and insect larvae. They're not just predators, they are also prey. Northern pike, largemouth bass, walleye, and yellow perch eat these small fish.

Fathead minnows use smelly signals to warn others about threats. They send chemical messages called pheromones to other fatheads. The scent messages might let others know they're injured or in danger. The smelly calls can bring more minnows and create a distraction. Then they can escape the predator.

Just as the fathead minnow sends messages for help, we can send our own calls—prayers. God hears each of our prayers, no matter how big or small. God always answers our prayers too. He answers with "yes," "no," or "not right now." Talk to God now and tell him what you want help with. He's listening.

Write about a time that God answered your prayer with "yes," "no," or "not right now." Then talk to God about how that made you feel.

Then you will call on me and come and pray to me, and I will listen to you.

JEREMIAH 29:12, NIV

Father, today I need ____________________________. Thank you for always hearing my prayers. In Jesus' name, amen.

Wild Wonder

People often use fathead minnows as bait when fishing.

Creature Connection

Create a food chain for a stream habitat. What do fathead minnows eat? Who eats the fathead minnows? And who eats those predators? Include photographs or drawings of these creatures in your food chain along with arrows to show what each one eats.

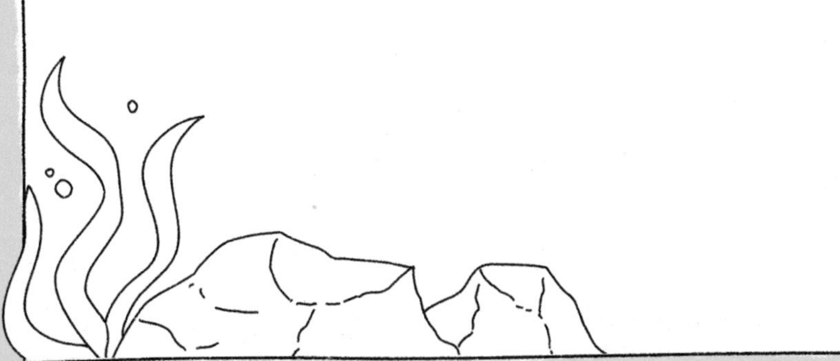

In the Wild

Visit a stream, creek, pond, or small river. In the shallow water search for minnows like fatheads. Use the photographs on these pages, an online search (with an adult's permission), or a field guide to try to identify what kind of minnow you see. What other wild wonders can you find?

Giant Seahorse

Scientific Name: *Hippocampus ingens*

Hold Tight

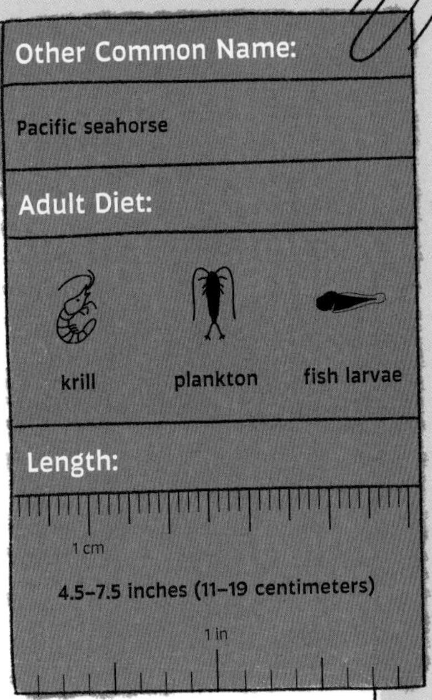

Other Common Name:
Pacific seahorse
Adult Diet:
krill
plankton
fish larvae
Length:
1 cm
4.5–7.5 inches (11–19 centimeters)
1 in

It may seem strange that a fish the length of your palm would be called giant, but some seahorses are the size of a lima bean. So *giant seahorse* makes sense.

Giant seahorses tend to be solitary fish. They swim upright and use their tube-like mouth to vacuum krill, plankton, and fish larvae into their mouths.

It's easy to assume all fish are good swimmers, but seahorses tire easily. They beat their back fin up to 70 times every second to get around. Their tiny pectoral fins help them balance and steer in the water. Unfortunately, when oceans become stormy, seahorses may be swept away—sometimes to their death.

Giant seahorses have color-changing skin (not scales) that helps them communicate. The different colors help them talk to potential mates. The male and female giant seahorses circle one another, almost like a dance. They flash colors and tangle their tails together. Days later, the female places up to 2,000 eggs inside the male's pouch. He fertilizes the eggs and keeps them safe for 2 weeks. The tiny babies hatch and live on their own.

Giant seahorses use their tails to grip branches of coral reefs to avoid drifting. By choosing something strong and rooted in the ocean floor, the giant seahorse usually stays safe. We might not get knocked down by ocean currents, but tough times do come. What you hold tight to matters. Jesus is our Rock, because he doesn't change. Rely on him during difficult times.

Ask an adult to help you find some more verses about relying on God. Write one or two favorites here.

Seahorses Are Fish?

Seahorses don't look like fish. They have a unique body shape, and they have no scales. Seahorses are weak swimmers. But they are fish. Like most other fish, seahorses have swim bladders to keep them floating, and they breathe through gills.

He alone is my rock and my salvation, my fortress; I shall not be greatly shaken.

PSALM 62:2

Jesus, I praise you for being my Rock who never changes. I know I can rely on you. In your name, amen.

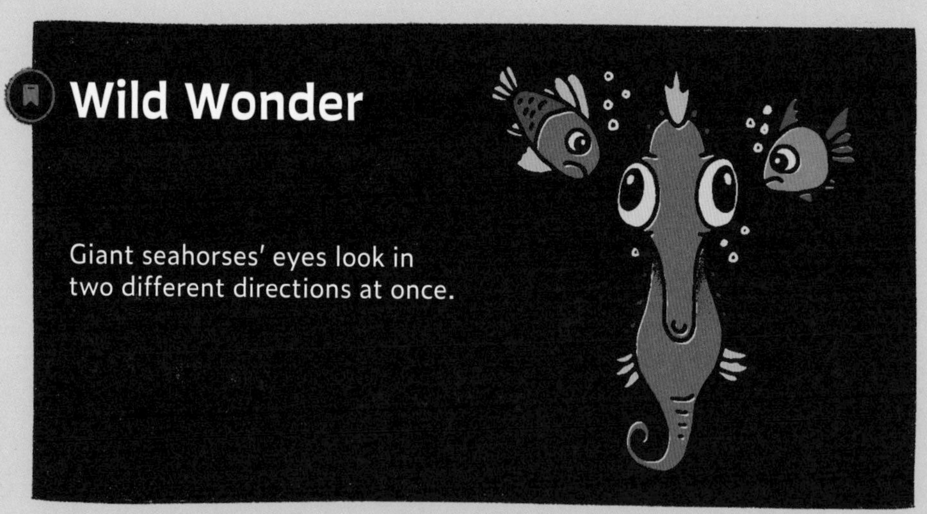

Wild Wonder

Giant seahorses' eyes look in two different directions at once.

Creature Connection

Create a seahorse from a chenille stem (pipe cleaner). Fold one end of the stem to create the horselike head. Continue folding for the body, and then wrap the stem around a pencil. When you use your seahorse pencil topper, it can remind you to cling tight to God.

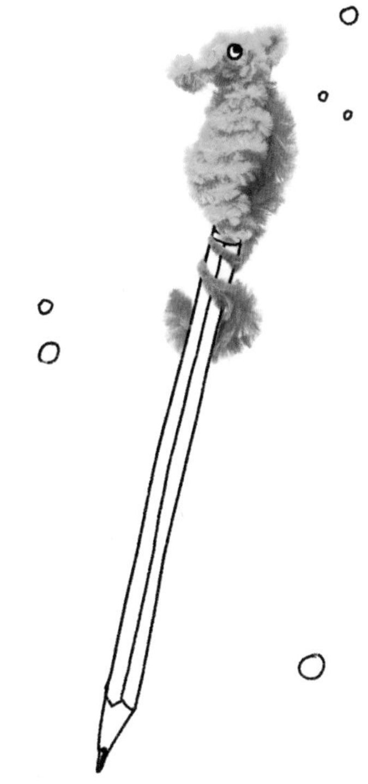

In the Wild

Gather some friends and family together on a warm day when they don't mind getting wet. Divide the group into two teams. Have each team hold the end of a long rope. Play a couple of rounds of tug-of-war. For the final round, turn on a sprinkler. It's harder to have a strong grip when your hands—and the rope—are wet (and you're not a seahorse with a strong tail).

Nopoli Rock-Climbing Goby

Scientific Name: *Sicyopterus stimpsoni*

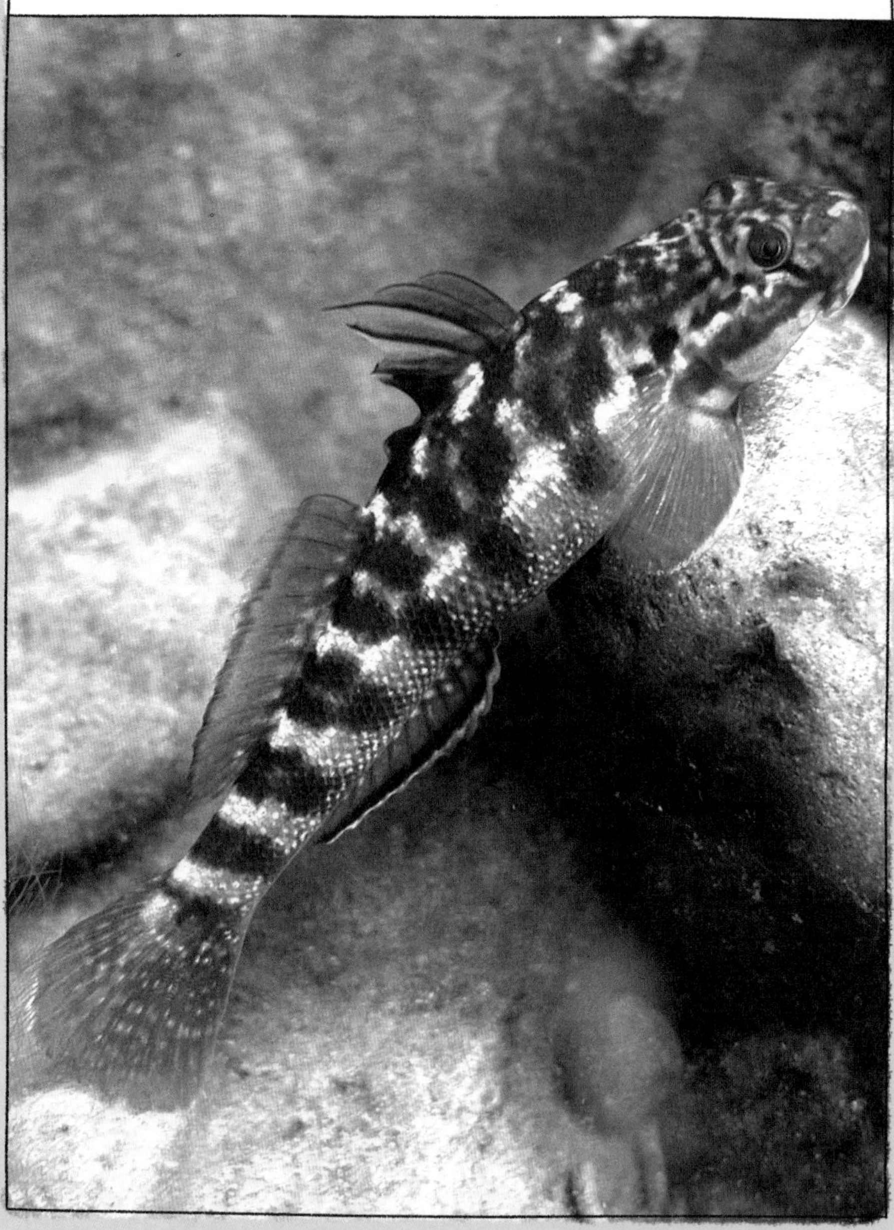

Rock Climber

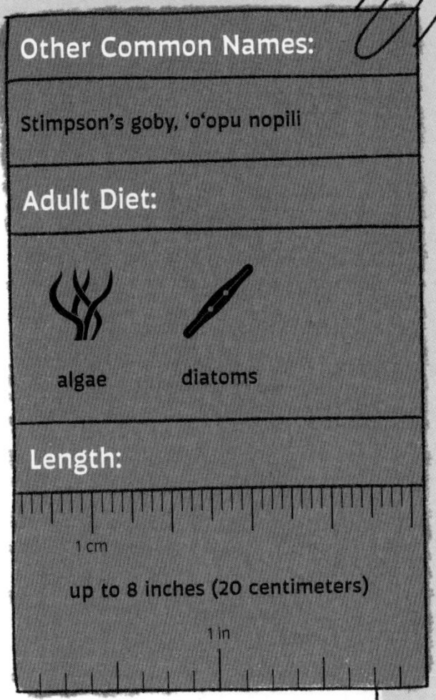

Nopoli rock-climbing gobies live in freshwater mountain streams on Hawaii's volcanic islands. During mating season, males turn brilliant blue with red and blue fins—quite different from their typical brown and black coloring. The females lay eggs in rock crevices to protect them in the fast-moving streams. Strong currents sweep the newly hatched larvae to the nearby saltwater ocean.

Later, the grown-up fish return to the freshwater streams to live. The Nopoli rock-climbing gobies defend their favorite feeding patches where they scrape and eat algae from rocks.

When hurricanes, flooding, landslides, or lava threaten their habitat, these fish need a new home. So, they move to a new stream with high-quality water. They even climb waterfalls to get there.

All gobies have an abdominal sucker made from their pelvic fins. The Nopoli rock-climbing gobies' mouths are a second sucker. Like mountain climbers, they scale Hawaii's waterfalls inch by inch until they reach their new home.

Nopoli rock-climbing gobies don't race to the top of waterfalls. Instead, they climb waterfalls as tall as 30-story buildings at a slow and steady pace. When a task feels too big for you, take it as slow as you need. For example, you might feel it's impossible to read the entire Bible. It's too long to read in a short period of time, but by reading just one paragraph, one section, or one chapter at a time, you accomplish something important: knowing God better.

What is a big task you would like to do to honor God? List all the smaller steps that will help you finish, slow and steady.

Let us not grow weary of doing good, for in due season we will reap, if we do not give up.

GALATIANS 6:9

Lord, help me to remember slow and steady Bible reading honors you. In Jesus' name, amen.

Wild Wonder

As they grow, Nopoli rock-climbing gobies' mouths move from the front of their heads to the underside of their heads—lower than most fish—but perfect for attaching to the rocks with suction.

Creature Connection

Get up close and personal to rocks like a goby fish. Use an egg carton to collect 12 rocks. Before adding a rock to your collection, clean and examine it. Look for its color(s), shape, and luster. (Luster means how shiny, dull, or sparkly it is.) Learn more about collecting rocks and rockhounding with a book or online source such as howtofindrocks.com (with an adult's permission). You can also learn more about rocks at dkfindout.com/us/earth/rocks-and-minerals.

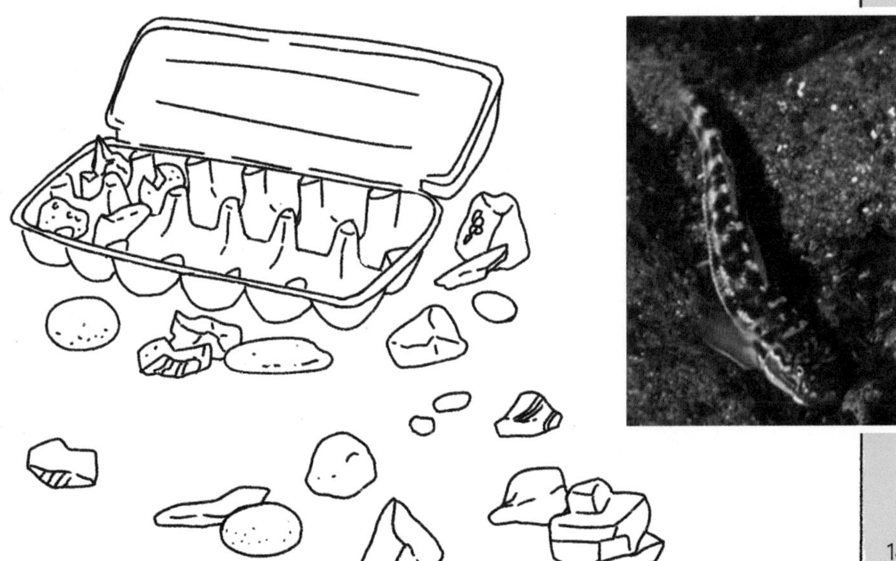

Flagtail Surgeonfish

Scientific Name: *Paracanthurus hepatus*

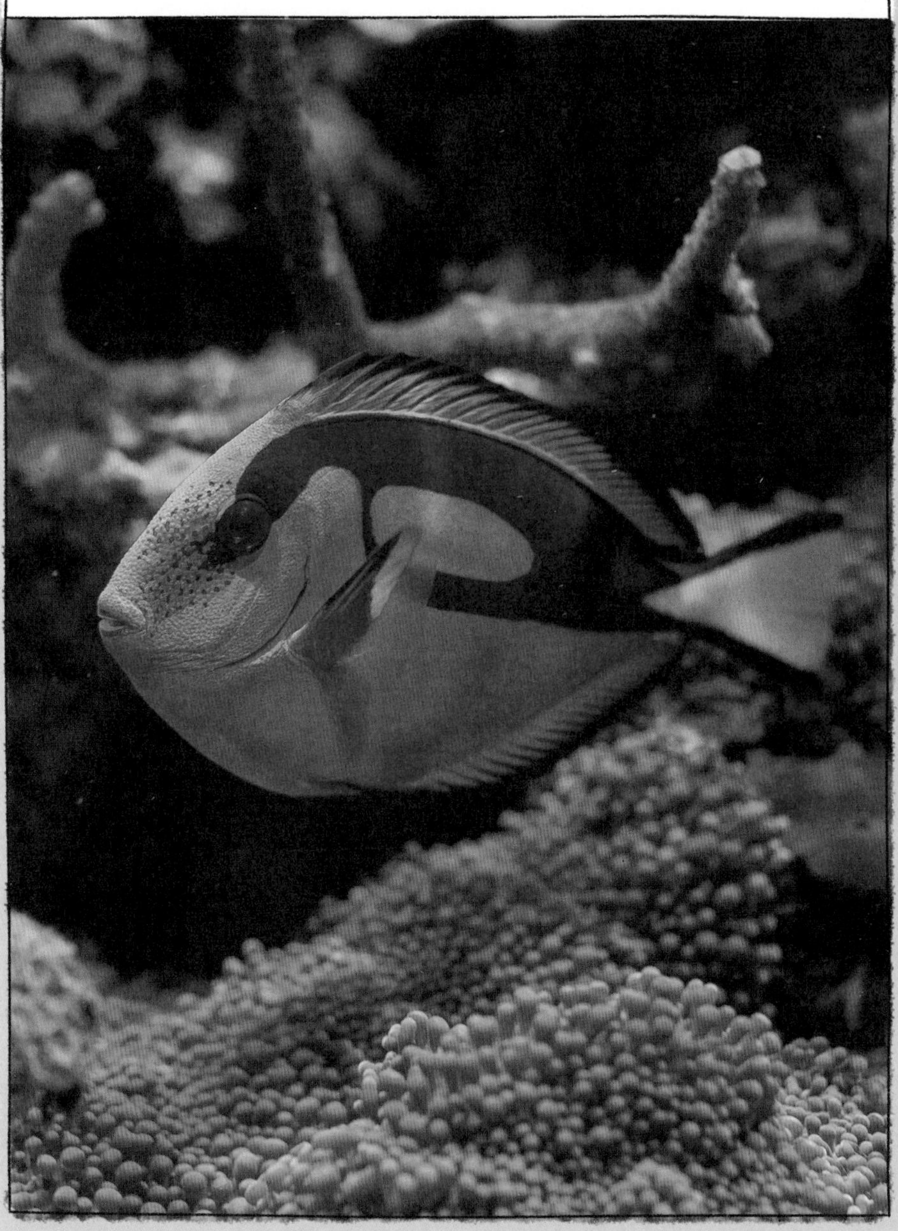

Grow with Light

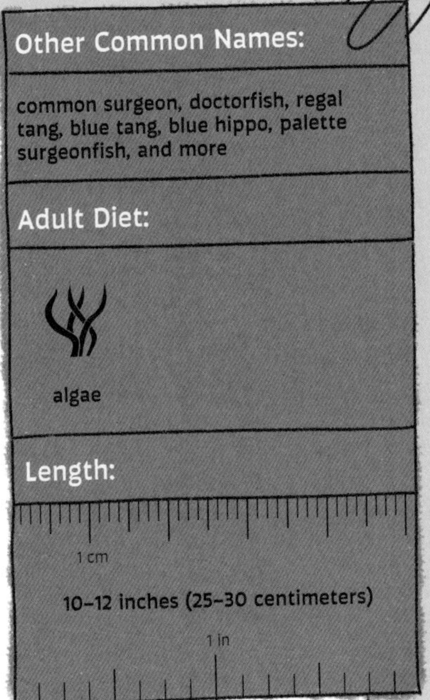

Other Common Names:
common surgeon, doctorfish, regal tang, blue tang, blue hippo, palette surgeonfish, and more
Adult Diet:
algae
Length:
1 cm
10–12 inches (25–30 centimeters)
1 in

Bright blue and yellow fish called flagtail surgeonfish often live in the tropics. They're mostly found in pairs and small groups. Coral reefs and rocks provide them a place to hide. The flagtail surgeonfish pull algae from the rocks and coral with their small teeth.

Flagtail surgeonfish cluster together in schools for protection. Their predators know not to hunt them, especially in large groups. Part of this fish's tail fin is a movable spine full of toxins. When threatened, the flagtail surgeonfish stabs the predator with the spine. The venom leaves the predator in significant pain as the flagtail surgeonfish swims to safety.

Flagtail surgeonfish hatch from eggs after just 26 hours—before they have enough time to fully form. Light helps them mature. Soon they have a heartbeat and grow quickly. Within 2 days their fins and eyes develop, and they begin to swim. These bright-yellow fish become blue as they grow up. And they mature without help from their parents.

How long it takes flagtail surgeonfish larvae to grow up depends on their exposure to light. Your maturity as a Christian is the same way. Jesus told us he is the Light of the World. Light helps you grow as a Christian. Without light we can't see where to go. Our Light—Jesus—helps us. He is our most important guide. Are you spending time with Jesus so you can grow and walk in his ways?

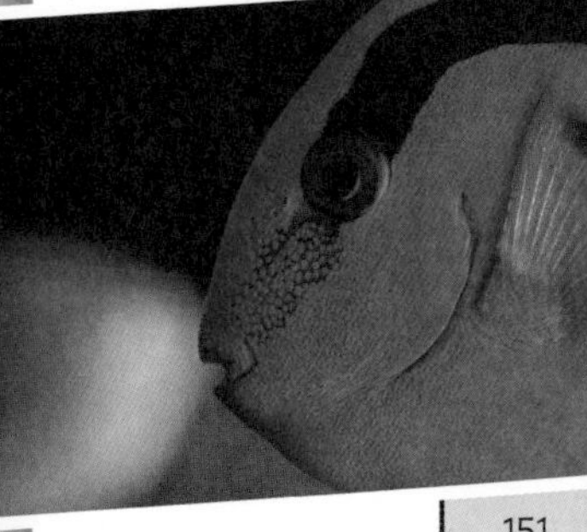

Talk to some trusted adults in your life about how they spend time with Jesus. Record their ideas so you can try them later.

Jesus spoke to them, saying, "I am the light of the world. Whoever follows me will not walk in darkness, but will have the light of life."

JOHN 8:12

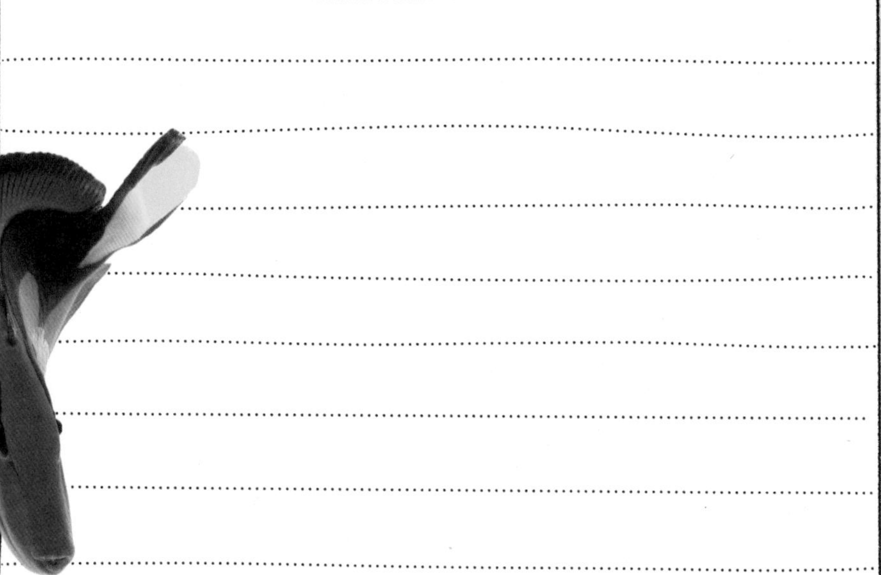

Jesus, thank you for being the Light of the World. Help me to spend time with you and go where you lead me. In Your name, amen.

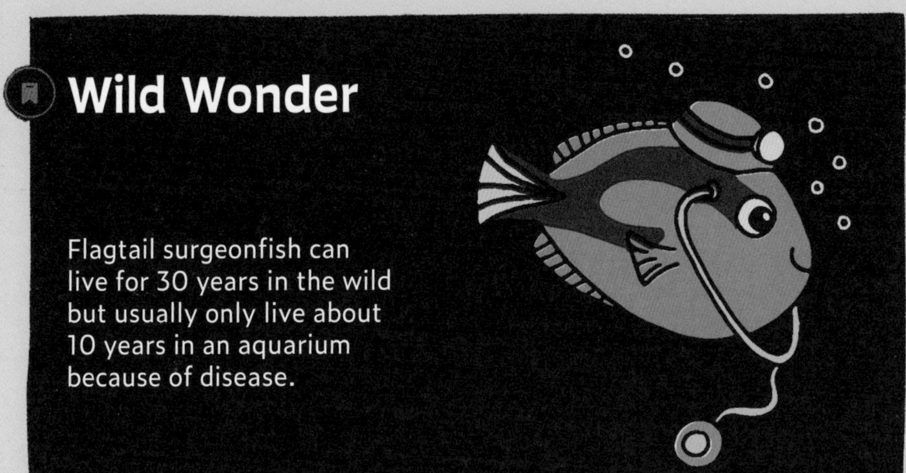

Wild Wonder

Flagtail surgeonfish can live for 30 years in the wild but usually only live about 10 years in an aquarium because of disease.

Creature Connection

The movies *Finding Nemo* and *Finding Dory* feature a flagtail surgeonfish. Try to learn more about the different species of fish featured in the movies. Which character is a flagtail surgeonfish?

Blobfish

Scientific Name: *Psychrolutes marcidus*

Puddle of Pudding

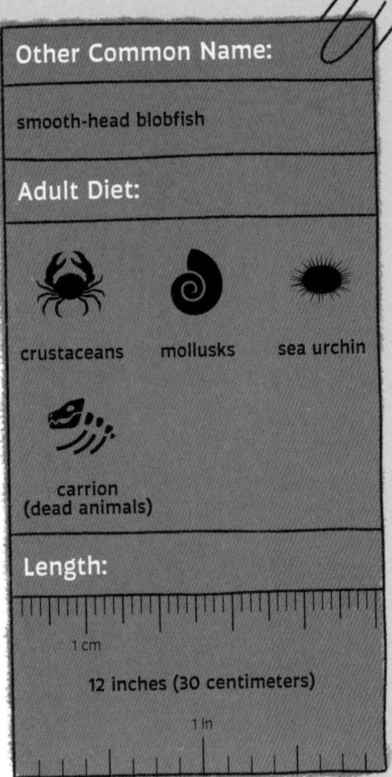

Other Common Name:
smooth-head blobfish
Adult Diet:
crustaceans
mollusks
sea urchin
carrion
(dead animals)
Length:
1 cm
12 inches (30 centimeters)
1 in

Off the coasts of Australia, Tasmania, and New Zealand, blobfish live in deep, deep waters. In their natural environment, blobfish look like other fish. But that changes when they come to the water's surface. Blobfish look more like a puddle of pudding at sea level than a fish.

Blobfish live 2,000 to 3,900 feet (600 to 1,200 meters) below sea level, where the water pressure can be 100 times stronger than at the surface. Their unique bodies help them survive the intense pressure. Loose skin covers their bodies. They have little muscle and soft bones.

Despite being a fish, blobfish don't really swim. They basically float along the seafloor without much effort. They eat crustaceans that float in front of them.

Scientists still have a lot to learn about blobfish. They're hard to study because they can only live at great depths in the ocean. Sometimes God can feel far away or hard to understand. But he wants us to know him—that's why he gave us the Bible. All the stories in the Bible tell one big story. It's the story of how God loves us and made a way to rescue us. When this world feels complicated, turn to God. Talk to him through prayer, and read the story he has written for you: the Bible.

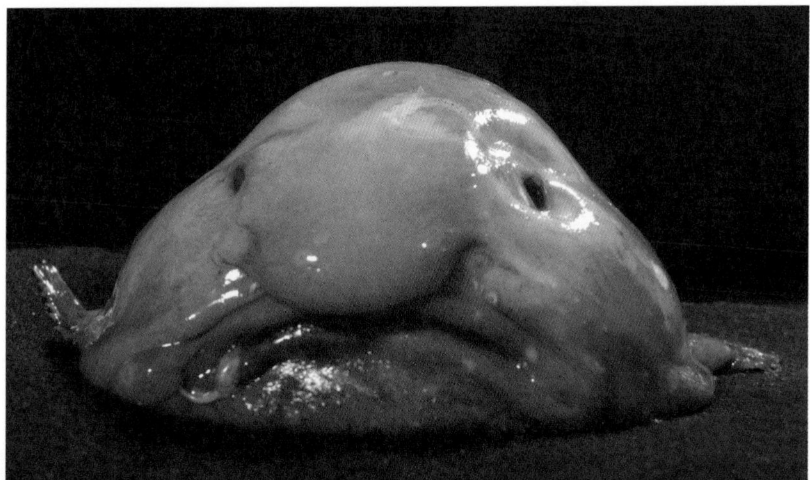

Does God sometimes feel far away or hard to understand? Write down a few things you've learned about God in the past year. Let your list encourage you to keep seeking him.

Your word is a lamp to my feet and a light to my path.

PSALM 119:105

Lord God, thank you for giving me your big story in the Bible. In Jesus' name, amen.

Wild Wonder

The scientists who found the first of this species of blobfish named it Mr. Blobby.

Creature Connection

Scientists need to learn more about blobfish through research. Think about a person, place, or thing you want to know more about. If you know the person, you can interview them. You might also read books and learn more online (with an adult's permission) about your topic.

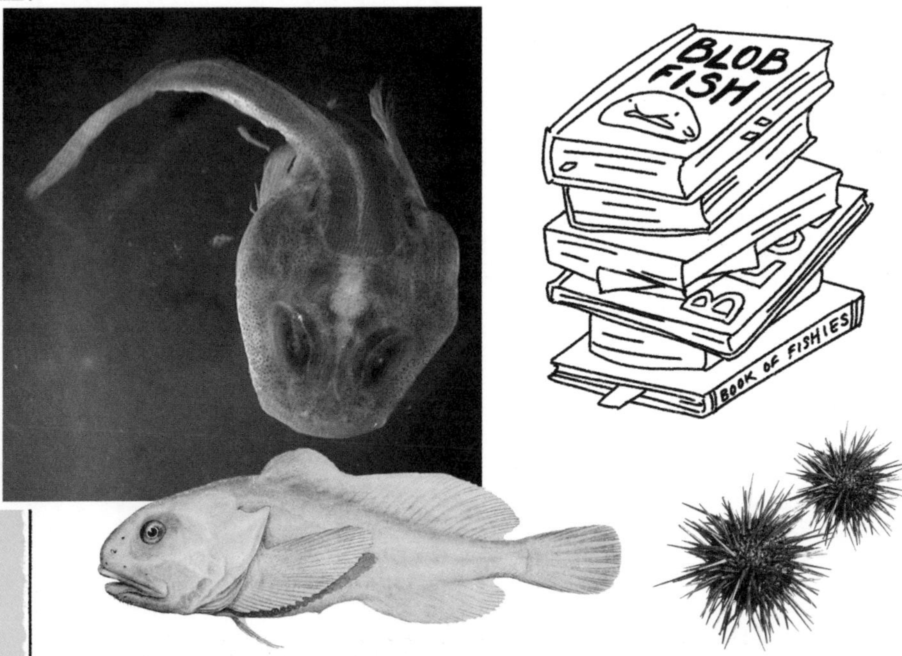

Reptiles have dry, scaly skin. We often see reptiles basking in the sun or moving to shade or water when they're warm because they are cold-blooded animals. This means they rely on their environment to warm and cool them.

After hatching from eggs, reptiles rarely receive parental care. About **12,000** reptile species live around the world. Most of these are lizards and snakes.

REPTILES

*

In the pages that follow, the length of these reptiles does not include the animals' tails. Scientists measure reptiles from their snout (nose) to vent (the opening near their tails often used to eliminate waste).

Marine Iguana

Scientific Name: *Amblyrhynchus cristatus*

Alarm Calls

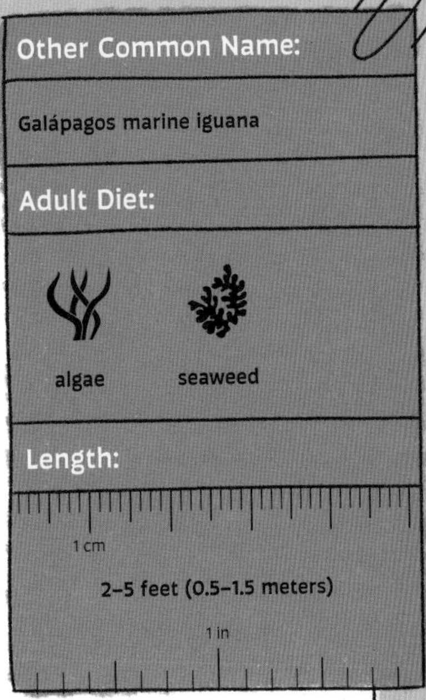

Other Common Name:
Galápagos marine iguana
Adult Diet:
algae
seaweed
Length:
1 cm
2–5 feet (0.5–1.5 meters)
1 in

Ferocious? Nah. Actually, the fierce-looking marine iguana is a gentle herbivore. It eats only underwater algae and seaweed. All those sharp teeth scrape algae from rocks. The long claws help it climb and cling to cliffs.

Marine iguanas can only be found on the volcanic islands of the Galápagos (off the coast of Ecuador). The islands are on the equator, but ocean currents make the water cold. So marine iguanas sunbathe in colonies on the rocks to get warm. These water lizards can dive more than 65 feet (20 meters) underwater for minutes at a time. Their long tails help them swim smoothly through the water. Although marine iguanas are fast on land, they are a bit clumsy.

When an island hawk predator flies overhead, marine iguanas might not see it when they're on the side of a cliff. But they still know it's coming. These lizards have learned to listen to another victim of hawks: mockingbirds. The marine iguanas usually ignore the songs of Galápagos mockingbirds, but when they hear the mockingbirds' alarm call, they pay attention. That's when these reptiles scramble into a crevice or under a rock until the hawk leaves.

Listening to birds keeps marine iguanas safe, and listening to others can keep you from harm too. Marine iguanas listen to their wildlife neighbors. Then they run for cover. Listen to wise friends and adults. Let their wisdom protect you.

Who are some wise adults and friends in your life? Usually these are people who know God well. Write down their names and commit to talking with one of them the next time you feel confused about what to do.

Listen to advice and accept instruction, that you may gain wisdom in the future.

PROVERBS 19:20

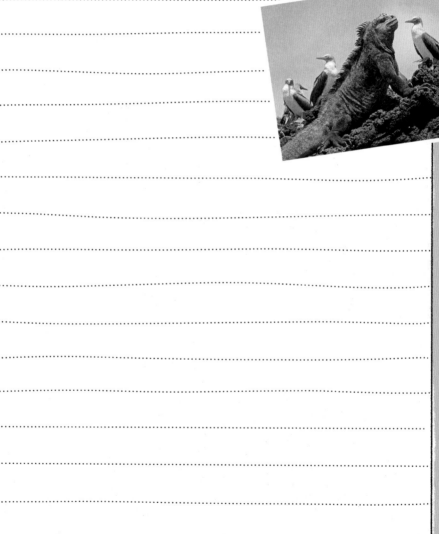

Heavenly Father, thank you for putting wise people in my life who protect me and give me good advice. In Jesus' name, amen.

Wild Wonder

Marine iguanas drink so much salt water that they sneeze out salt.

Creature Connection

The marine iguana knows the difference between the Galápagos mockingbirds' songs and alarm calls. With permission, go online to listen to a mockingbird's song and calls. (The video found at allaboutbirds.org/guide/northern_mockingbird/sounds is a good place to start.) Can you hear the difference?

MOCKINGBIRD SONG

Common Garter Snake

Scientific Name: *Thamnophis sirtalis*

Hidden Eggs

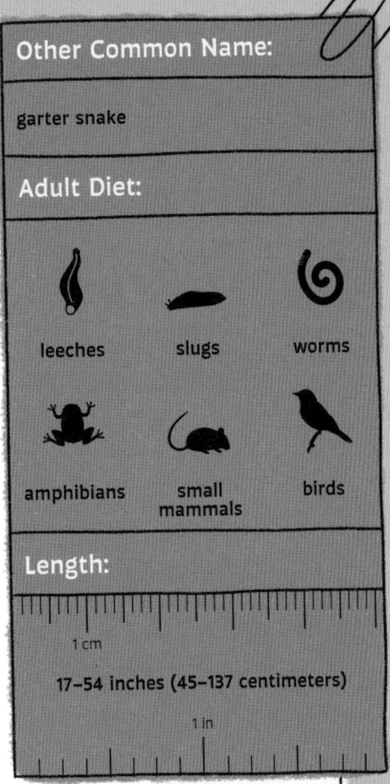

The common garter snake has 3 light-colored stripes on a greenish, brown, or black body. Garter snakes live throughout North America. You might spot them near streams, lakes, or swamps. They're also in forests, fields, and city parks. Though they feast on slugs, frogs, and worms, they're basically harmless to people.

As reptiles, garter snakes hatch from eggs, but females don't *lay* eggs. Instead, the eggs incubate inside the female's abdomen. After 2 to 3 months, 10 to 40 little snakes are born. Though some are as small as 4 inches (10 centimeters), they are independent from birth.

Common garter snakes use touch and smell to communicate with one another. Mostly, they learn about their world through their forked tongue. Tipped in black, their tongue collects information, especially chemicals, from the air—like a nose.

Ssss! A garter snake flicks out its tongue. It tastes the air. Then it pulls the tongue inside and touches the tongue to the 2 sensory pits in the roof of its mouth. These pits analyze the information.

Garter snakes use their tongues to explore the world around them through smells. You explore with your senses too. Your tongue tastes food—but that's not all. You also use your tongue to talk. When it comes to the words we say, speaking with honesty and kindness is just as important as the words we choose. When we do that, our words are sweet to others—and to God.

What are some "sweet" words you could say to a friend or family member?

Gracious words are like a honeycomb, sweetness to the soul and health to the body.

PROVERBS 16:24

Lord God, thank you for words. Help me to use them in kind and honest ways. In Jesus' name, amen.

Wild Wonder

Young garter snakes shed their skin about once a month to keep up with their rapid growth.

Creature Connection

Use play dough to create a baby snake along with some small animals that snakes eat. Pretend the snake eats the small critters. Each time the snake "eats," add the critter play dough to the snake and watch it grow.

In the Wild

Make a snow snake outside. Place basketball-sized snowballs next to one another in a slithering line. Smooth out the balls so they form the body of the snake. Add a head and tail. Decorate the snake with unsweetened dried fruit (like raisins) or unsalted nuts to give the animals that come to your yard a winter treat. If you have access to a beach or sandbox, you could also make a sand snake.

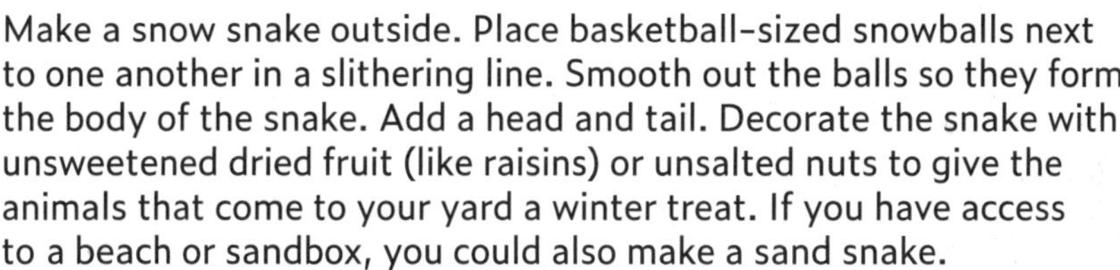

Texas Horned Lizard

Scientific Name: *Phrynosoma cornutum*

Squirting Blood

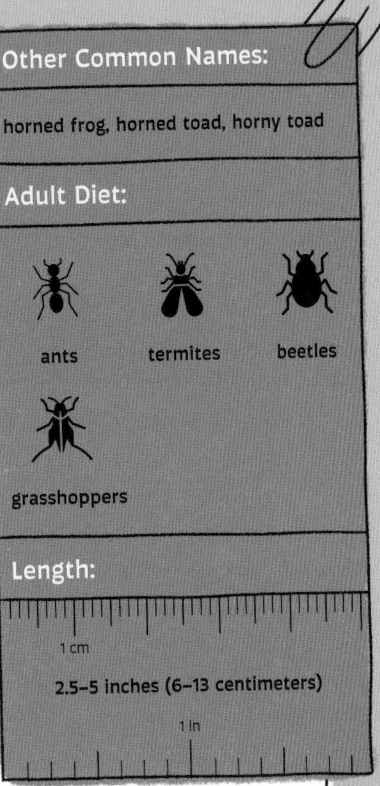

You might find a Texas horned lizard sunbathing on the open prairie or in the desert. Their wide, flat bodies are good for digging, so at night they bury themselves in the sand or soil to sleep. Horned lizards have a toad-like body, which is why some people have nicknamed them horned toads. Don't be fooled; they're lizards.

Texas horned lizards have a few ways to protect themselves. Their red, brown, or gray spiky skin helps camouflage them in their environment. They'll also puff themselves up, which makes them big, with their scales sticking out so they are tough to swallow.

These lizards have another way to save themselves from predators such as the pygmy owl, coyote, or western diamondback rattlesnake. They squirt blood from their eyes. They take aim and fire a stream of blood up to 5 feet (1.5 meters)! Predators like wolves and dogs don't like the chemicals in this blood.

It's often the blood of the Texas horned lizard that saves its life. A different blood saves us. In the Old Testament, God required animal sacrifices to pay the price of sins. But God planned from the beginning to send his Son to earth as the final sacrifice. Jesus bled and died on the cross. He paid the penalty for our sins by shedding his innocent blood for us. No other blood is needed.

Write down two or three ways Jesus' death on the cross has changed your life. Talk with an adult if you aren't sure.

If we walk in the light, as he is in the light, we have fellowship with one another, and the blood of Jesus his Son cleanses us from all sin.

1 JOHN 1:7

God, thank you for giving your Son for me. Jesus, thank you for dying to save me. In your name, amen.

Wild Wonder

The horns of the Texas horned lizard are made from bone—not skin.

Creature Connection

Go outside to use a water gun or spray bottle to squirt water at a small, empty plastic container (like a yogurt or cottage cheese tub). Try to move or knock the container over by squirting water at it. How far away can you stand and still move the container?

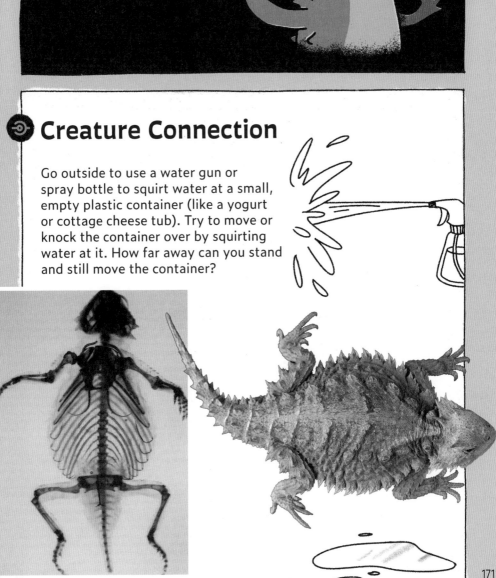

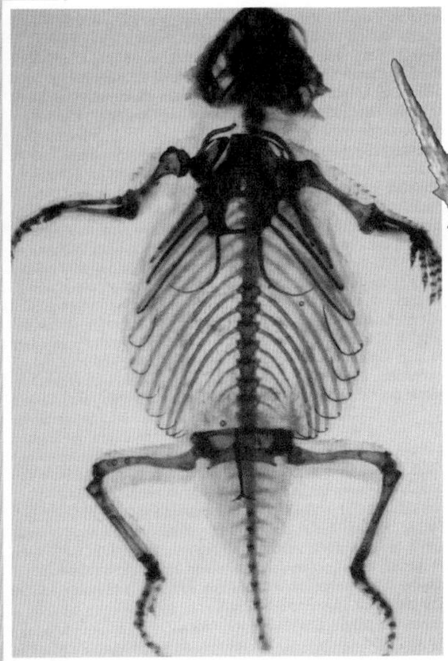

American Crocodile

Scientific Name: *Crocodylus acutus*

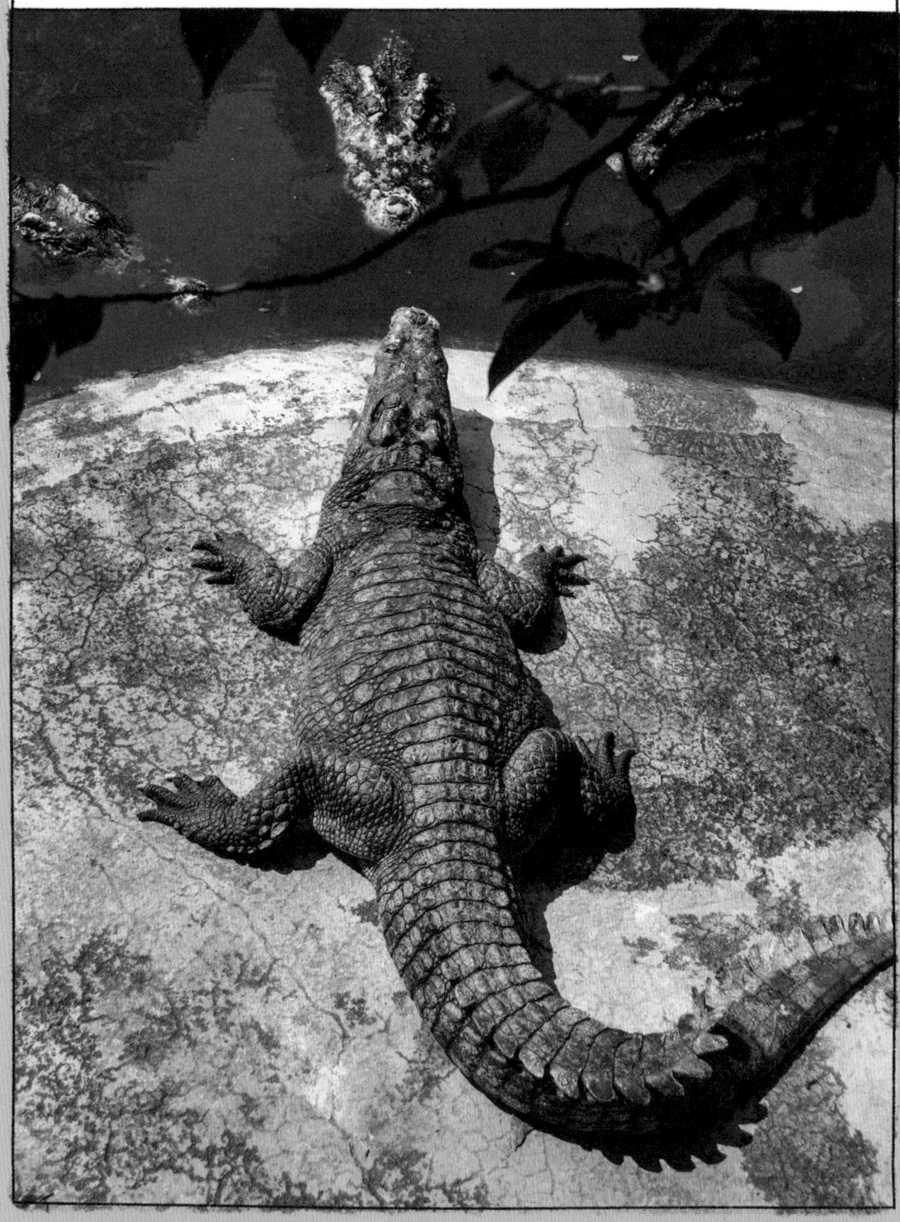

After a While, Crocodile

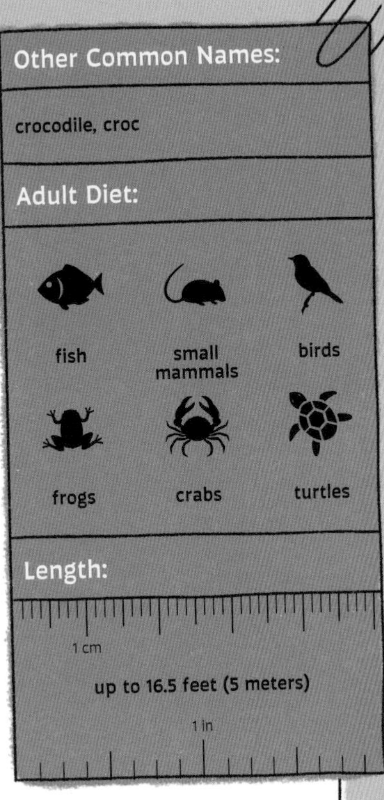

American crocodiles live in the brackish and salt waters of Florida as well as Central and South America. A clear protective eyelid allows them to keep their eyes open underwater. These huge reptiles bask in the sun with their mouths wide open. Their gaping mouths help them to cool down.

These crocodiles dig complex burrows that are partially underwater. The burrows shelter the crocs from cold weather and give them a place to rest.

Crocodiles spend most of their time in the water, but they lay eggs on land in giant nests. The female crocodile places between 30 and 60 eggs in the nest to incubate and covers them with sand or dirt. Later, she returns to the nest and listens for signs of the eggs hatching. When it's time, she uncovers the nest and helps the hatchlings climb out of their eggs. The male and female both guard the hatchlings until they take the babies to water after a couple of weeks. Once in the water, the young crocodiles fend for themselves.

Most reptiles don't take care of their babies, but American crocodiles watch their eggs and care for the young hatchlings. We can choose to be different from others too. Even if a lot of people think or do something, you don't have to go along with it. Just as God created the crocodiles to care for their young, he created you to do good in the world. He wants you to obey his words and follow him, not the crowd.

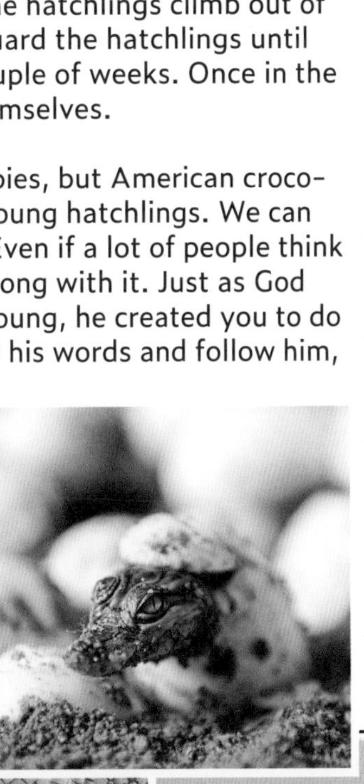

Croc or Gator?

Alligators and crocodiles are part of the order Crocodylia and are closely related. Here are a few differences when considering all species of crocs and gators.

Crocodiles	Alligators
HUGE! 6–20 feet (2–6 meters) long	Really large! 8–13 feet (2.5–4 meters) long
Narrow V-shaped snout	Wide U-shaped snout
Bottom and top teeth visible when mouth closed	Only top teeth visible when mouth closed
Found in North and South America, Africa, Australia, and Asia	Found only in the United States and China
Rarely seen in the United States	Often seen in the southeastern United States

It can be hard to act differently from your friends. Plan ahead by writing down one or two situations where you might be tested and what you will do in those situations.

Do not be conformed to this world, but be transformed by the renewal of your mind, that by testing you may discern what is the will of God, what is good and acceptable and perfect.

ROMANS 12:2

Dear God, help me to obey your words and follow you even when my friends do not. In Jesus' name, amen.

Wild Wonder

The American crocodile can live up to 100 years, though most live 60 to 70 years.

Creature Connection

Crocodiles growl deeply when defending themselves or their young. Think about what it might sound like, and then listen to croc sounds online with an adult's permission. Do crocodile sounds remind you of any other creatures?

THREAT CALL

HATCHLING CALL

Painted Turtle

Scientific Names: *Chrysemys dorsalis*, *Chrysemys picta*

A Hard Shell

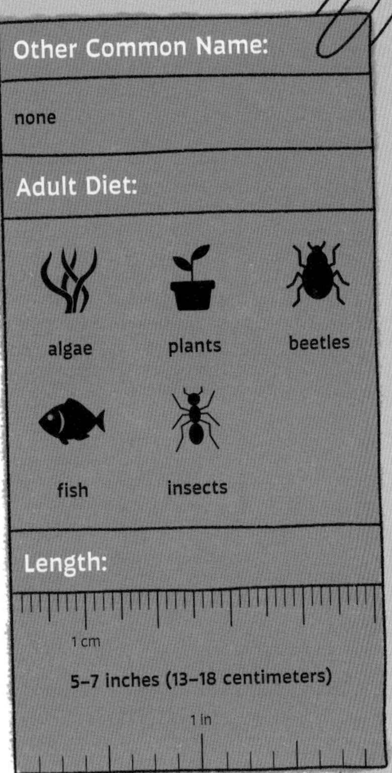

The painted turtle's hard shell provides protection from predators like otters, raccoons, mink, and foxes. The upper shell, called a carapace, is dark green or black. It has red, orange, or yellow markings.

The turtles' aquatic homes in ponds, marshes, and slow rivers have plenty of plants and muddy bottoms. In the winter they burrow into the mud to hibernate.

These reptiles soak up sunshine while basking on logs and rocks. They keep watch while sunning themselves, so if enemies—or you—approach, the turtles dive into the water. Another defense mechanism they have is pulling their legs and head inside their shells. Some painted turtles can live as long as 35 to 40 years, though it's usually less.

The water isn't just for safety. These omnivores munch beetles, algae, and more in the water. Painted turtles don't have teeth, but their jaws have horny plates that help them grip food. Since their tongues don't move much and they don't make saliva, they have to eat in the water. The water helps the food move down their throat for digestion.

Turtles' attached shells go everywhere with them. Like a football player's pads or a soldier's helmet, a turtle's shell acts as a kind of armor to keep it safe. Ephesians 6:14-17 talks about the armor of God. It includes the belt of truth, the breastplate of righteousness, the gospel of peace shoes, the shield of faith, the helmet of salvation, and the sword of the Spirit. God equips us with his armor to protect our minds and hearts. Remember God's armor each day when you get dressed.

Which piece of God's armor do you feel most in need of today? Why?

Take up the whole armor of God, that you may be able to withstand in the evil day, and having done all, to stand firm.

EPHESIANS 6:13

Heavenly Father, thank you for protecting my mind and heart with your armor. In Jesus' name, amen.

Wild Wonder

When hibernating, turtles breathe through an opening in their butts called a cloaca.

In the Wild

Visit a pond, lake, or stream on a sunny day. Walk quietly and slowly while watching for turtles sunning themselves on rocks, logs, or even in the grass. You may want to take binoculars so you can watch from a distance without scaring the turtle.

Creature Connection

Draw a turtle using the photographs from these pages as examples. When adding details, make sure the turtle's shell has at least 6 segments. Write each of the pieces of the armor of God on a separate segment of the turtle's shell, and then hang the drawing near your closet or dresser.

King Cobra

Scientific Name: *Ophiophagus hannah*

Nest Builder

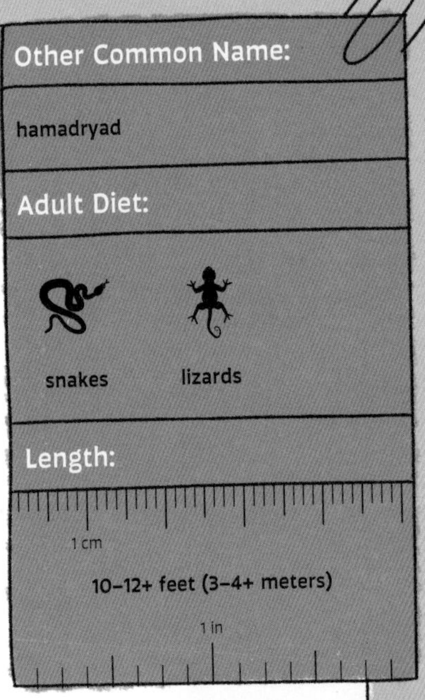

Other Common Name:
hamadryad
Adult Diet:
snakes
lizards
Length:
1 cm
10–12+ feet (3–4+ meters)
1 in

When provoked, king cobras hiss and flare out their hoods. They also raise most of their 12-foot-long (4-meter) bodies to appear threatening. These long snakes may be fierce and aggressive, but they prefer to escape a fight.

But the snakes need to eat. King cobras feast on other snakes, especially large ones like Asian rat snakes and pythons. King cobras look dangerous—and they are. They may not be the most venomous snake in the world, but one bite has enough venom to kill an elephant or many people. The venom affects the victim's breathing and causes heart failure. Quick medical treatment is necessary to prevent death. Thankfully, they're a bit shy and try to avoid people.

King cobras are also very protective of their young. They're the only snakes that build a nest for their eggs. They push leaves, twigs, and branches into a nest pile. The female lays about 20 to 40 eggs. Then the male and female king cobras guard the nest until black hatchlings emerge.

Just as king cobra parents defend their eggs, God protects you. He promises to always guard, care for, and comfort you because he loves you. King David wrote about being scared in the Psalms, but he always remembered that God was with him. Knowing that helped David, and it can help you too. Talk to God the next time you are afraid.

List some things you feel afraid of. Then talk to God about each one, asking him to protect you.

The LORD is my light and my salvation; whom shall I fear? The LORD is the stronghold of my life; of whom shall I be afraid?

PSALM 27:1

Dear God, thank you for your comfort and promises of protection. In Jesus' name, amen.

Wild Wonder

King cobras raise their heads so high they can look you—or even an adult—in the eye.

Creature Connection

Draw a snake's head in the center of a piece of colored paper. From one side of the head, continue to draw the snake's body in a spiral. Cut along the lines you drew and give your snake eyes. Cut a tongue from black paper and tape or glue it to the snake head. Attach a string to the head. Tie the string to a craft stick and make the cobra stand up.

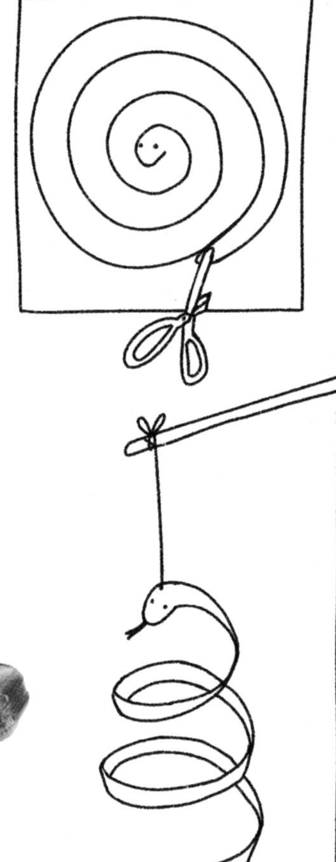

Panther Chameleon

Scientific Name: *Furcifer pardalis*

Wide-Eyed View

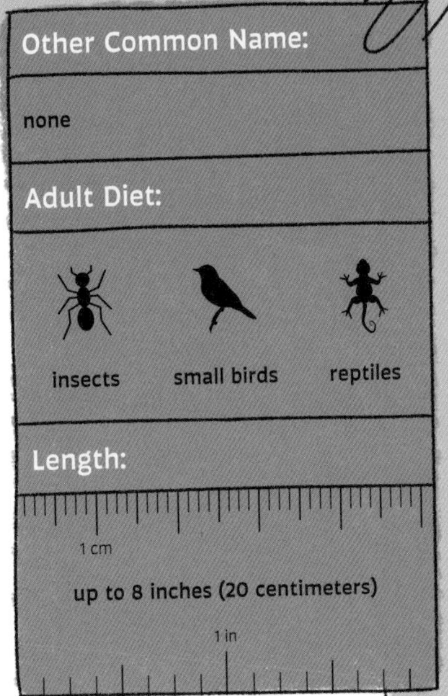

Other Common Name:
none
Adult Diet:
insects
small birds
reptiles
Length:
1 cm
up to 8 inches (20 centimeters)
1 in

Off Africa's coast, panther chameleons live on the island of Madagascar. These chameleons display a rainbow of colors including brown, blue, green, red, orange, purple, turquoise, and pink. These vibrantly colored lizards change their color in less than 30 seconds to attract mates, communicate, and regulate their body temperature.

Skin color changes also help panther chameleons to camouflage themselves. They don't want a predator or their prey to see them. As they wait, their eyes rotate in 2 different directions at once. This gives them a wide view of everything. Once they find their next snack, they focus both eyes on it. Then . . . snatch!

The attack is fast and precise, using the panther chameleon's amazing tongue. Sometimes longer than the chameleon's body, the tongue's tip is like a suction cup. And it's so sticky and strong, the prey can be up to one-third of the chameleon's body weight. Imagine snatching a 25-pound (11-kilogram) burger with just your tongue. That's practically what the panther chameleon does—but on a smaller scale.

Panther chameleons are always watchful. We should be too. God is doing great things in our lives. A small blessing from God might be your teacher recognizing your hard work. Another gift might be a smile from a kid on the school bus. But look for big blessings too. New friendships, a visit with grandparents, or volunteering in your community. The greatest gift of all is Jesus saving us from our sin. Keep watching for God's good gifts.

Think back over your week. Try to remember and write down one blessing from each day.

Every good gift and every perfect gift is from above.

JAMES 1:17

Jesus, you are the greatest gift of all. I love you. In your name, amen.

Wild Wonder

Chameleons have forked feet that help them keep a tight grip on small branches.

Creature Connection

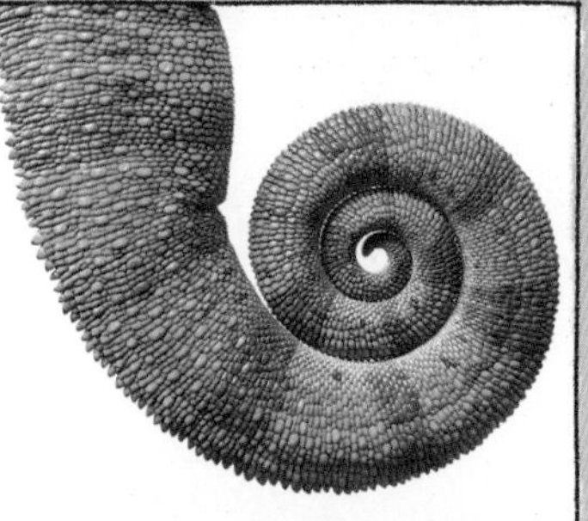

Decorate a jar with a drawing of eyes to remind you to be watchful like a panther chameleon. Write down a gift from God on a small piece of paper every day. Place the papers in the jar. Your blessing jar can be just for you, or your whole family can contribute daily. At the end of a month, read over all the blessings in the jar.

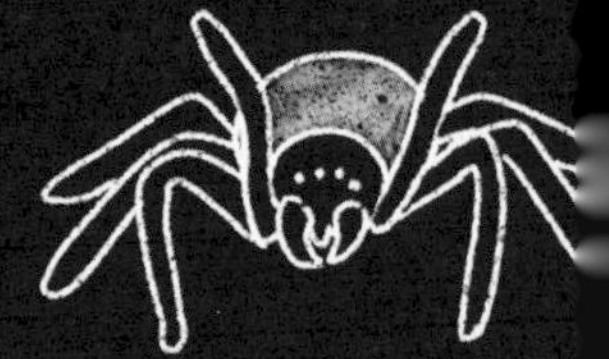

More than **50,000** species of spiders live throughout the world. With 8 quick legs and venomous fangs, they're known as skilled predators. Yet 99.9 percent of spiders do not have bites that are life-threatening to people.

All spiders pull silk from their spinnerets, which are silk-producing organs. They use silk to protect their eggs and wrap prey. Many spiders also build webs, but some spiders have other ways to locate prey.

SPIDERS

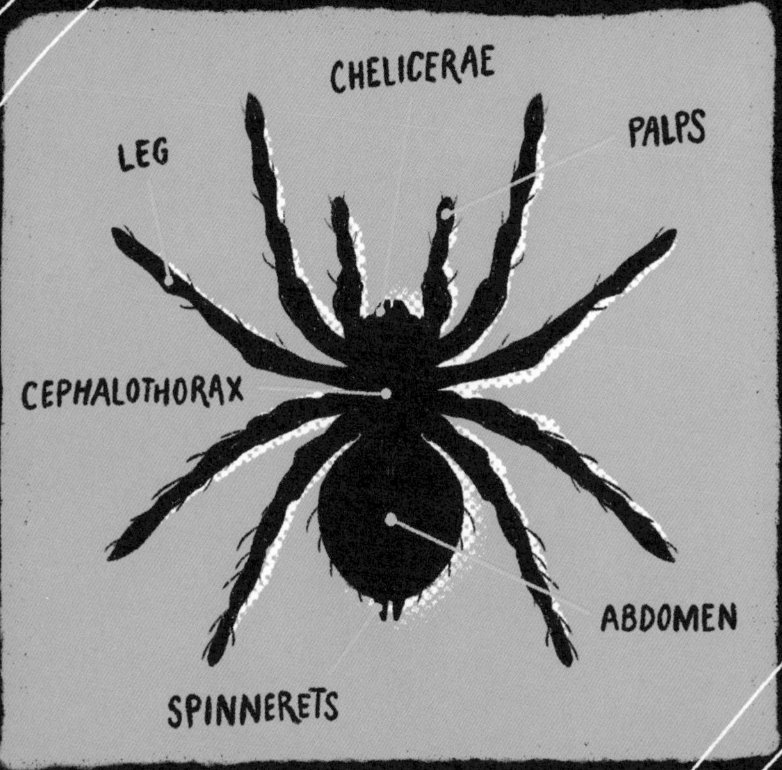

CHELICERAE
LEG
PALPS
CEPHALOTHORAX
ABDOMEN
SPINNERETS

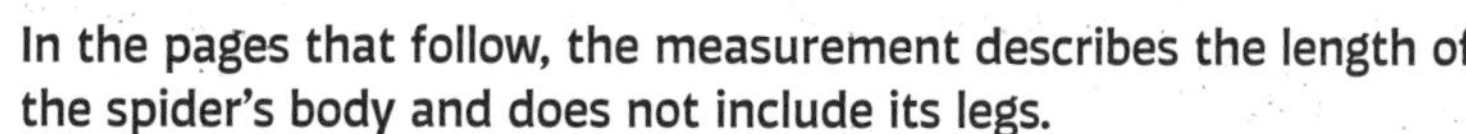

In the pages that follow, the measurement describes the length of the spider's body and does not include its legs.

Peacock Spider

Scientific Names: *Maratus sceletus*, *Maratus jactatus*, *Maratus robinsoni*, and more

Bold Beauty

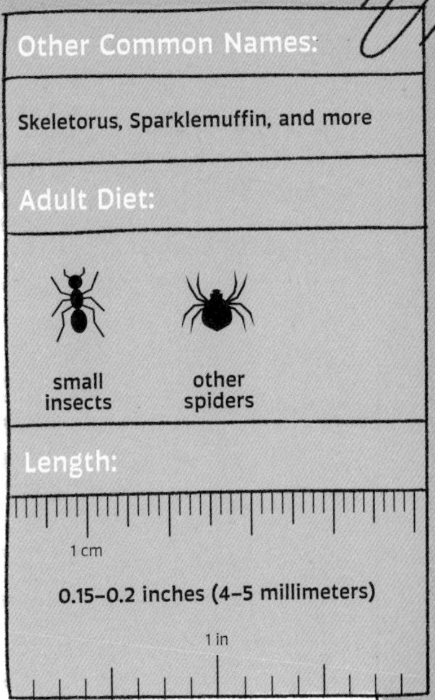

Other Common Names:
Skeletorus, Sparklemuffin, and more
Adult Diet:
small insects
other spiders
Length:
1 cm
0.15–0.2 inches (4–5 millimeters)
1 in

Named after the vibrant bird, peacock spiders are brightly colored—if they're male. Scalelike hairs in red, orange, white, and blue form a variety of patterns. But female peacock spiders tend to be plain brown in color.

Peacock spiders are a group of jumping spiders. They're tiny—just 4 to 5 millimeters in length—but they sure do jump! To avoid a predator, they can jump 40 times their body length. Peacock spiders are native to Australia, and they live in various habitats like sand dunes, grasslands, and leaf litter.

These spiders move and hunt constantly. A male uses his bold colors and dancing to get the attention of a female. He waves his third pair of legs and his colorful tail flap. This tiny peacock spider can dance for nearly an hour to get the female's attention.

Male peacock spiders persist with their dancing. They want a mate, so they don't give up. When it comes to matters of faith, be like the peacock spider. Trust God and continue to obey him. Don't give up. Keep on praying and talking to God, even when you don't understand why things happen the way they do.

Is there an activity or situation God wants you to persist in, even if it's hard? Write about it here.

Blessed is the one who perseveres under trial because, having stood the test, that person will receive the crown of life that the Lord has promised to those who love him.

JAMES 1:12, NIV

Jesus, thank you for helping me to keep trusting and following you, even when I don't understand everything that happens. In your name, amen.

Wild Wonder

Most spiders have poor vision, but peacock spiders see well.

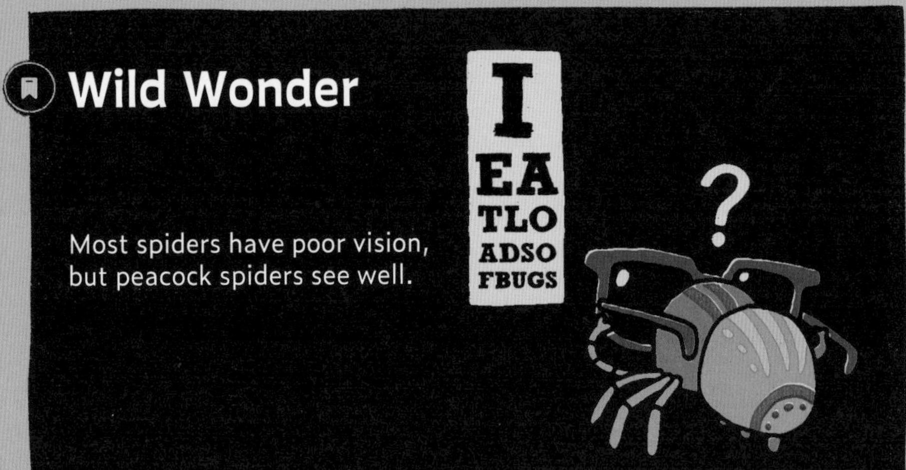

Creature Connection

With an adult's permission, watch a video of a jumping spider's dance, such as this one: pbs.org/wnet/nature/peacock-spider-attracts-mate-with-colorful-dance/15763. Then practice dancing like a jumping spider. As you dance, wave your arms and flutter a fan.

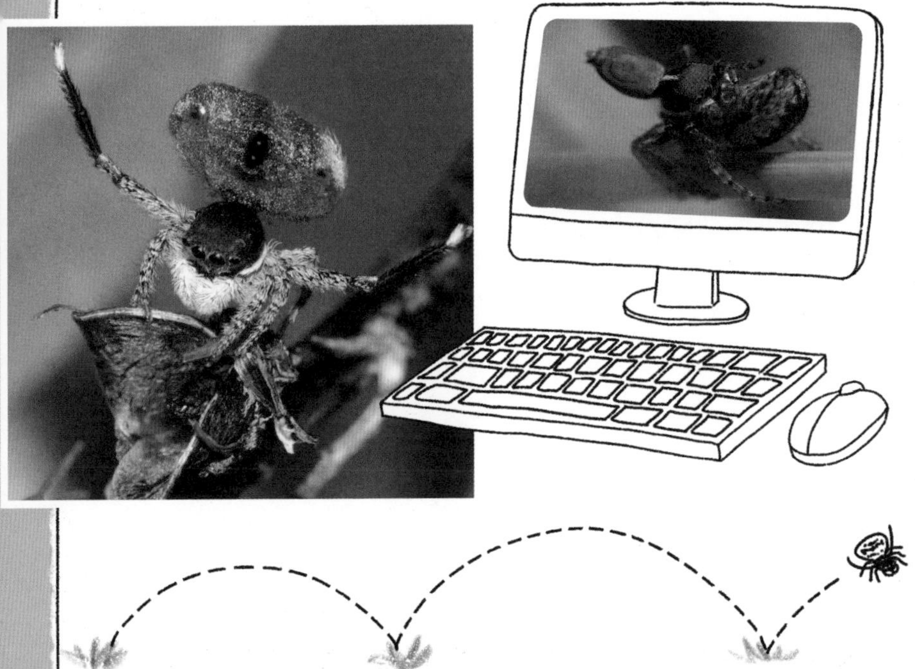

Diving Bell Spider

Scientific Name: *Argyroneta aquatica*

Deep Diver

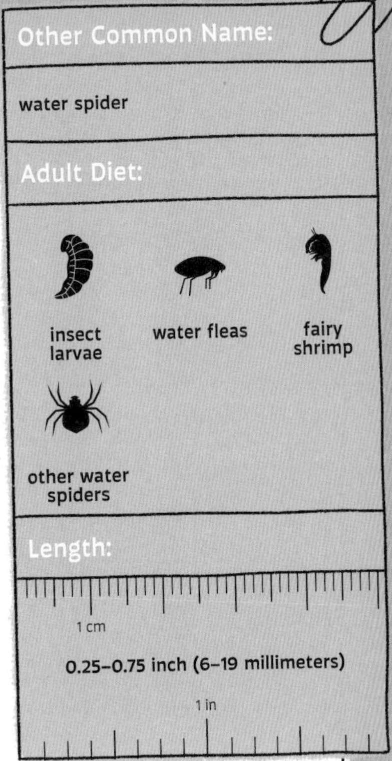

Just one spider lives entirely underwater. It's the diving bell spider.

These spiders hatch from eggs underwater. They eat, grow, and molt underwater. They mate and lay eggs underwater. Diving bell spiders do all of this in their silk nests that are—you guessed it—underwater. So how do these spiders breathe? They weave a silk nest attached to a water plant and fill it with a big air bubble.

The diving bell spider returns to the surface of the water to get air when the nest needs more oxygen. It's usually about once a day. After collecting air bubbles on the hairs of its abdomen, it returns to the nest to add the new air to its underwater home.

God designed diving bell spiders to live underwater even though they need oxygen like other spiders. As Christians, we live in a world that tries to make us think we need stuff more than we need God. Think about what keeps your faith healthy. When the world feels like it's getting too loud, ask God to remind you how much you need him. Spend some time with God today.

What are some warning signs that you feel overwhelmed or like the world is too much? Make a list so you can recognize the problem and choose to spend time with God.

Do not love the world or the things in the world. If anyone loves the world, the love of the Father is not in him.

1 JOHN 2:15

Heavenly Father, you are what I need most. Help me to love you. Thank you. In Jesus' name, amen.

Wild Wonder

A female diving bell spider dangles her front legs outside of her nest until she senses—and snatches—her prey.

Creature Connection

Make your own diving bell. Fill a large, see-through bowl partway with water. Turn a clear glass or cup upside down. Lower the glass straight into the water. If the cup stays straight, you can see the trapped air inside it—like in the diving bell spider's nest.

The Other Diving Bells

Before scuba gear was available, people explored underwater in open-bottomed containers that trapped air inside. It's thought that even Alexander the Great used one of these diving bells hundreds of years before Jesus was born.

House Spider

Scientific Names: *Parasteatoda tepidariorum*, *Achaearanea tepidariorum*

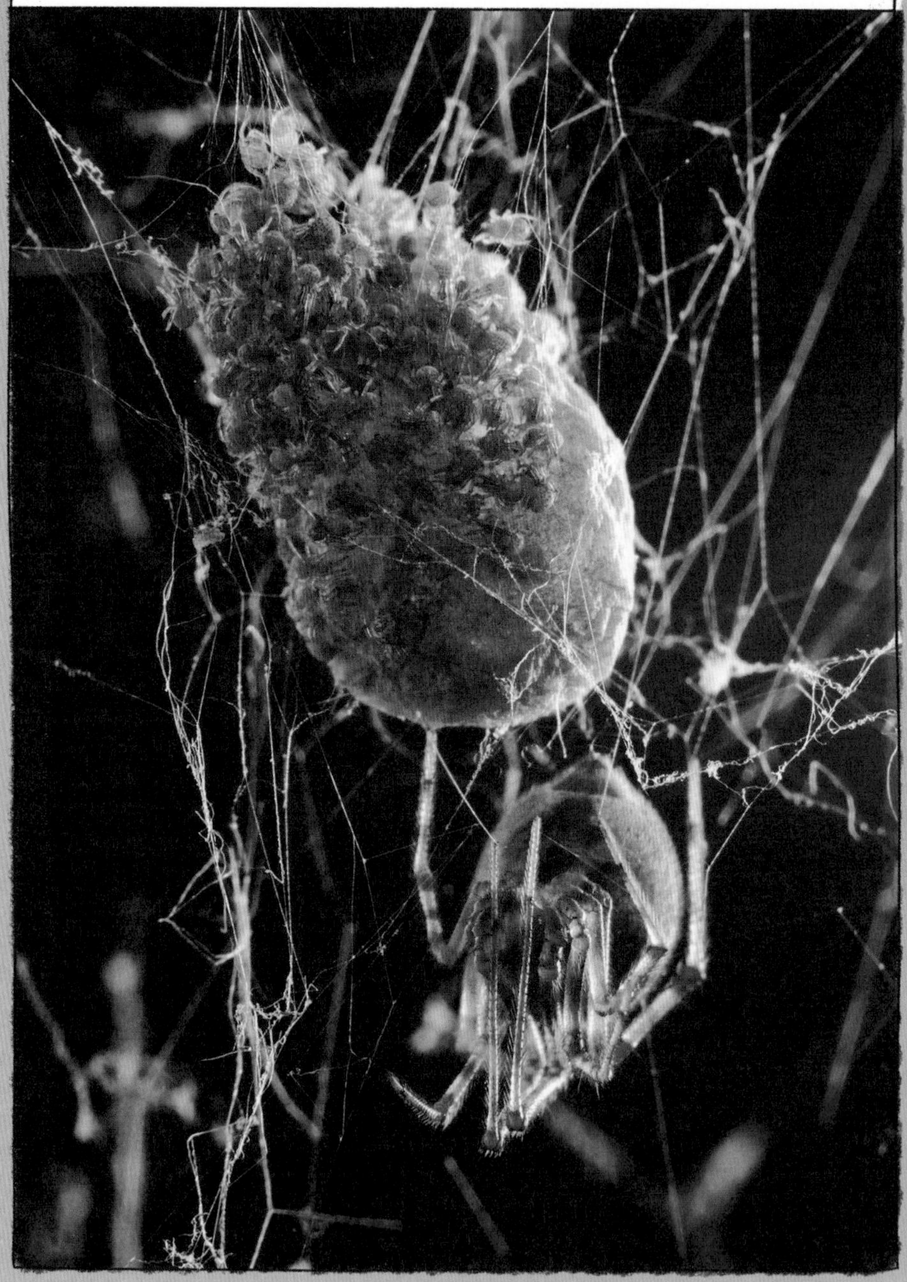

Houseguest

House spiders live all over the world. Likely one has set up home—a cobweb—in your house. House spiders build webs in the corners of closets, barns, and fence posts. They prefer to live inside (or near) buildings instead of in the wild.

These spiders build large, messy webs of tangled strands of silk. House spiders spend most of their time catching food in their web.

The house spider hangs upside down on its web. When a visitor climbs inside the web, it becomes trapped. The house spider first paralyzes the victim. Then it spins the prey with its second and third pair of legs while wrapping it in silk. The house spider might eat it right away . . . or save it for later.

Though people don't always love living with spiders, they're helpful to us. The house spider gets rid of insect pests like mosquitoes, flies, and cockroaches that invade our homes. God created all the animals, including house spiders. By respecting his creation, we honor God. Since house spiders are not dangerous to us and rarely bite, if you see one in your closet or garage, consider leaving it there. It can be your very own house-guest, but it will make its own bed and catch its own dinner, unlike typical company.

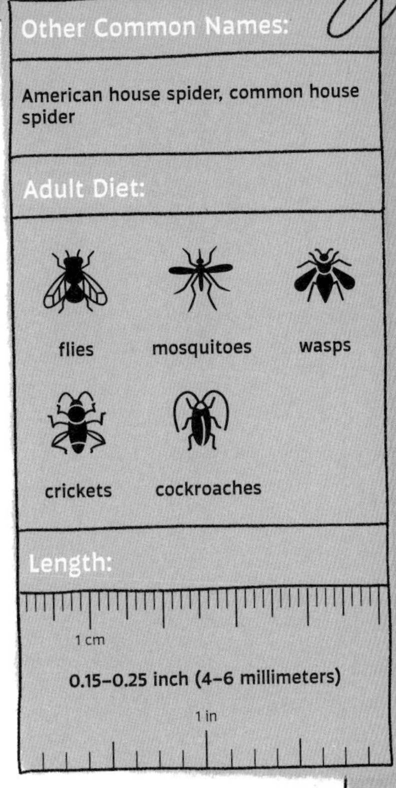

Other Common Names:
American house spider, common house spider
Adult Diet:
flies
mosquitoes
wasps
crickets
cockroaches
Length:
1 cm
0.15–0.25 inch (4–6 millimeters)
1 in

Take a look out a window or around your yard. Write down all the things you see that God created beautifully. Thank him for them.

God said, "Let the earth bring forth living creatures according to their kinds—livestock and creeping thing and beasts of the earth according to their kinds." And it was so.

GENESIS 1:24

God, thank you for making the world so beautiful and including spiders in it. In Jesus' name, amen.

Wild Wonder

House spiders are predators of scorpions.

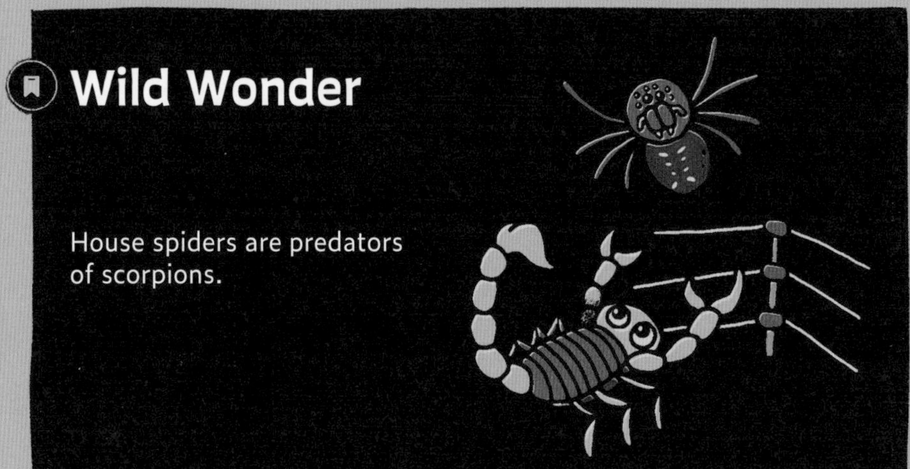

Creature Connection

Look around your home for a spiderweb. You might look in dark basement corners, under beds, and in closets. You can even look outside near doorways and windows. Quietly watch the web for several minutes. Did you spot the spider? If not, take a blade of grass (or something similar) and lightly touch the web to see if it gets the owner's attention. Leave the spider and web safe. You might even name the spider.

Daddy Longlegs Spider

Scientific Name: *Pholcus phalangioides*

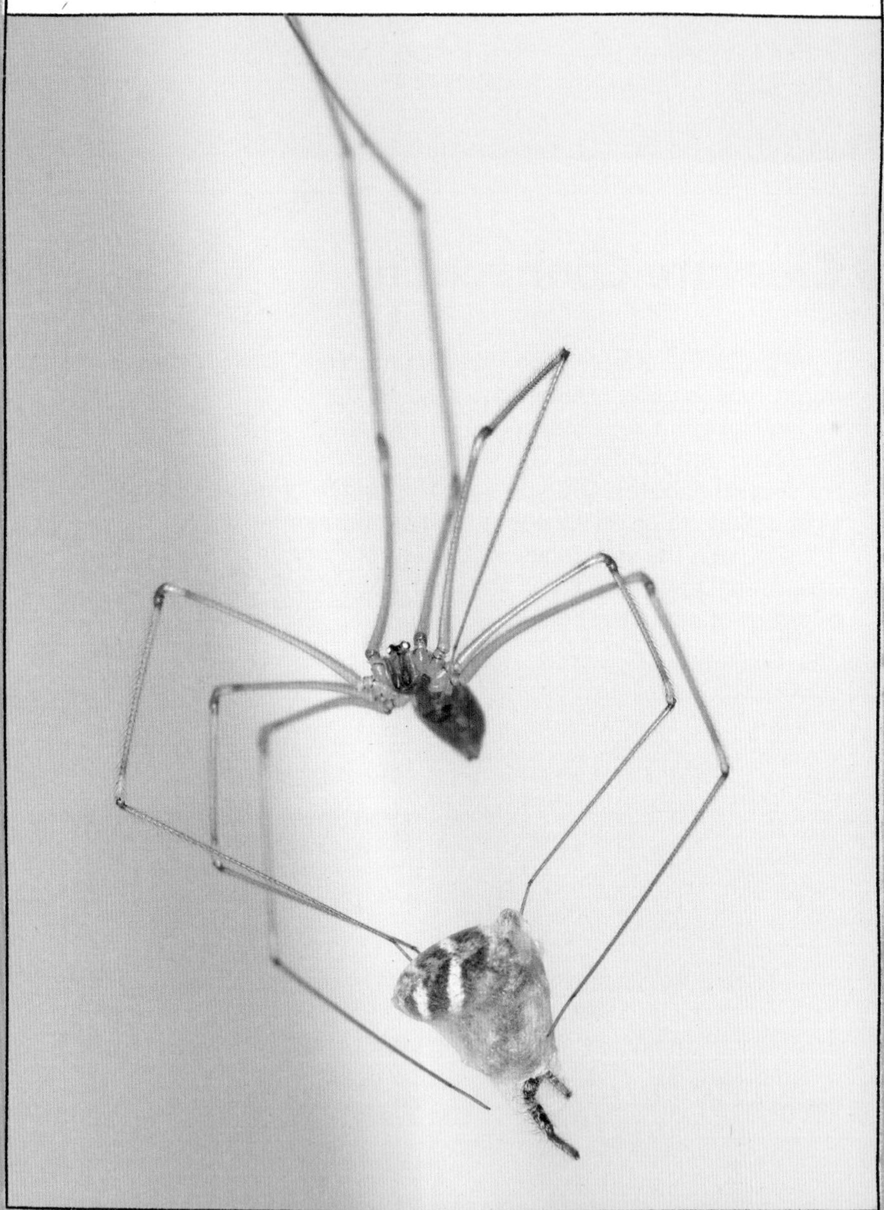

An Impostor?

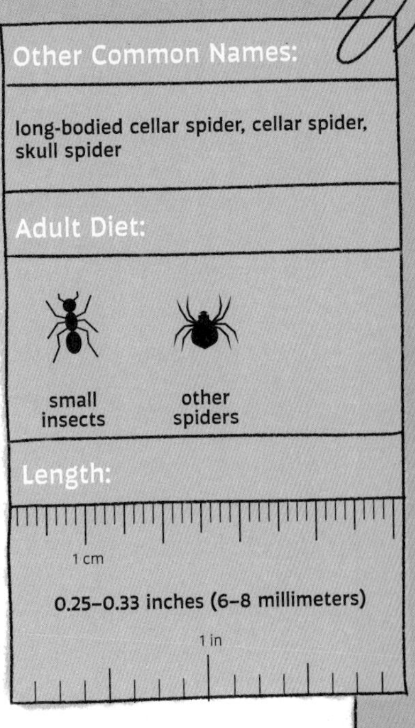

Other Common Names:
long-bodied cellar spider, cellar spider, skull spider
Adult Diet:
small insects
other spiders
Length:
1 cm
0.25–0.33 inches (6–8 millimeters)
1 in

Daddy longlegs spiders typically live indoors. They prefer quiet, dark corners where they can be left alone. Their large webs are made of silk, but these webs are not sticky. Instead, the spider hangs upside down, waiting for prey inside the loose silk strands of its web. The daddy longlegs throws silk over its victim. Then, the daddy longlegs might dine right away or save the insect for later.

Sometimes, the daddy longlegs spider even hunts other spiders, including ones that can be dangerous to people. In order to catch them, it just needs to be a faster or better hunter than that spider. But it won't hurt you!

All spiders are arachnids, but there are other arachnids that aren't spiders, such as mites, ticks, and scorpions. One non-spider arachnid is commonly mistaken for a spider. Its scientific name is *Leiobunum vittatum*, but its common name is the harvestman or daddy longlegs. The daddy longlegs spider has the scientific name *Pholcus phalangioides*. Since the two arachnids look similar and have similar common names, it can be confusing—but the scientific names help us keep them straight.

Using scientific names for animals prevents mistakes and confusion, especially since there are about 50,000 species of spiders around the world. The scientific name is the official name for an animal. Names are important in the Bible too. God tells us his many, many names in his Word. It's important to only use God's name when you are talking to him or about him. If you sometimes say his name as an expression, ask God to forgive you and to help you stop.

With permission, do an online search of the names of God and their meanings. Make a chart here to show some you want to remember.

> You shall not misuse the name of the LORD your God, for the LORD will not hold anyone guiltless who misuses his name.
>
> **EXODUS 20:7, NIV**

Lord God, help me to keep your name sacred by using it to honor you. In Jesus' name, amen.

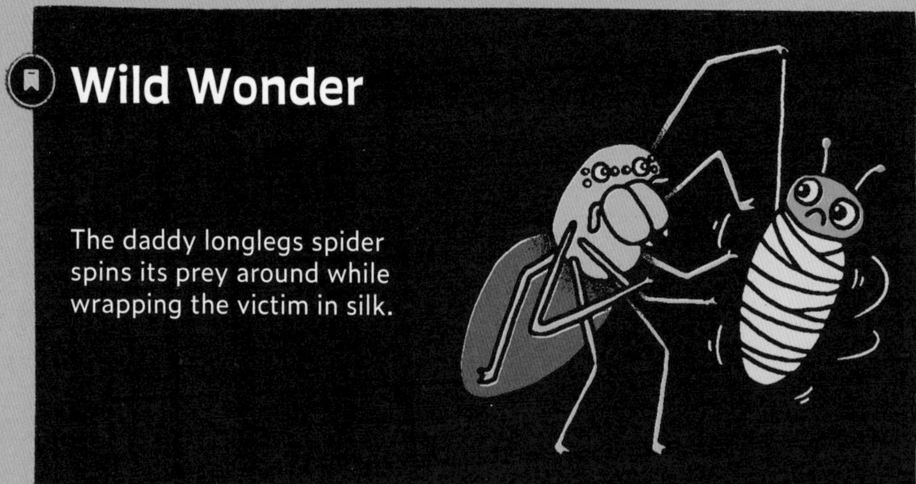

Wild Wonder

The daddy longlegs spider spins its prey around while wrapping the victim in silk.

Creature Connection

Choose your favorite name for God from the previous page and write it in decorative letters along with its meaning.

Wolf Spider

Scientific Name: *Hogna carolinensis*, *Pardosa milvina*, *Tigrosa helluo*, and more

Piggyback Style

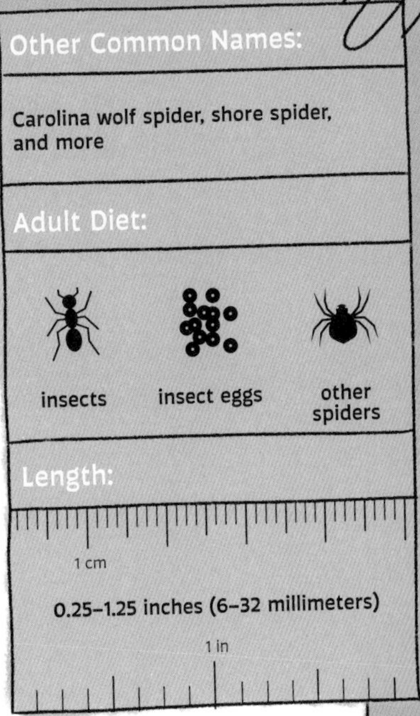

Other Common Names:
Carolina wolf spider, shore spider, and more
Adult Diet:
insects
insect eggs
other spiders
Length:
1 cm
0.25–1.25 inches (6–32 millimeters)
1 in

The most common spider on earth can be found across much of the world, from the freezing Arctic to the hot subtropics. Wolf spiders live in forests, fields, and gardens. Most wander without a permanent home. Others build burrows with holes or tunnels in the soil.

Wolf spiders can be black, brown, or tan. Their long legs make them extra fast and agile. There are thousands of wolf spider species, and even experts cannot always tell the difference between them without a microscope.

Only a few wolf spider species build webs to capture food. Instead, some try the sit-and-wait approach, anticipating their next meal will eventually come to them, and then they can attack. Other wolf spiders chase down their food. Their 8 eyes watch in all directions. Then the chase is on. With great speed they catch up with their prey and then—pounce!

Female wolf spiders are one of the few spider species that care for their young. The mother attaches her egg sac to her spinnerets and carries her eggs with her—even when hunting. When the spiderlings emerge from the eggs, they climb on their mother's back. About 100 baby spiders ride piggyback for a week or more.

Wolf spiders catch their meals in a variety of ways. Often there are multiple ways to do something. When it comes to memorizing Bible verses or other challenging activities, you might need to try several methods before finding success. Ask family or friends for ideas to help you achieve your challenge while relying on God to meet all your needs through his strength.

Can you think of something you'd like to do that seems hard? Write your ideas on how to do it here, along with any suggestions from friends or family.

I can do all things through him who strengthens me.

PHILIPPIANS 4:13

Father, thank you for giving me strength through your Holy Spirit. In Jesus' name, amen.

Wild Wonder

Baby wolf spiders (and other species) find new homes by "ballooning." They catch the wind on a strand of silk.

Creature Connection

Test your back strength. Find 30 or more items that are about the size of your hand and not fragile. A box of crayons, an action figure, or a rock might work. Place 10 of these items in a backpack. Try on the backpack and notice its weight. Keep adding more items. Though 10 items may not be heavy, adding more weight and keeping the backpack on for a long time will tire your muscles.

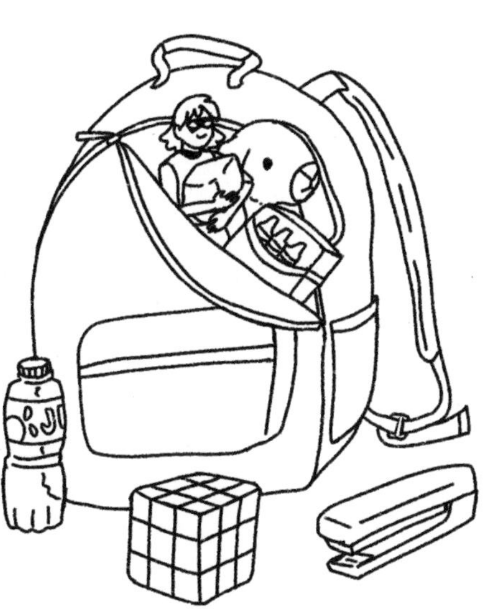

Goliath Bird-Eating Spider

Scientific Name: *Theraphosa blondi*

Giant Goliath

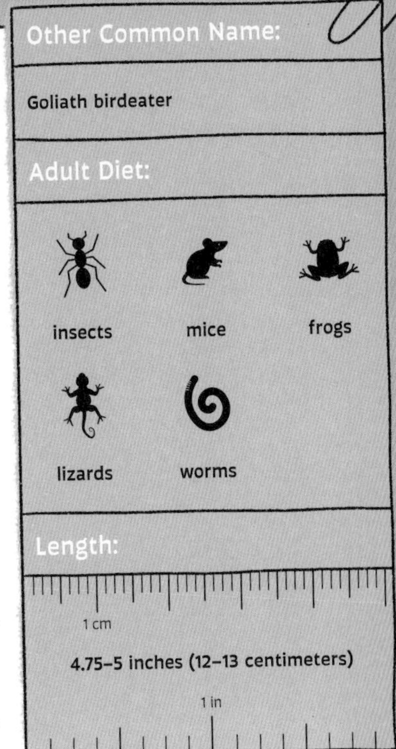

In the rain forests of South America, the Goliath bird-eating spider hunts at night. It uses stealth to ambush its prey. With a quick bite, this tarantula uses venom to turn the victim's insides to liquid. Then the Goliath bird-eating spider sucks the carcass dry. Only skin and bones remain.

The Goliath bird-eating spider has the heaviest body of any spider in the world. Its legs span about 12 inches (30 centimeters). It feasts on small critters like insects, mice, and lizards. (It rarely hunts birds, despite its name.)

When frightened, most spiders run away. Not Goliath bird-eating spiders. They rear up on their hind legs and rub their hairy legs together to create a hissing sound. They even flick hairs from their abdomen and hind legs. These barbed hairs stick in the attacker's skin, mouth, and eyes and cause pain and itchiness. But these spiders attack only when they feel threatened.

The Goliath bird-eating spider knows how to fight to protect itself when danger comes. Usually it's unwise for people to fight, but if a bully bothers you or someone nearby, you can courageously tell the bully their actions are wrong. Jesus didn't fight the people who were cruel to him, but he stood up to the Pharisees, who were religious bullies. David stood up to Goliath, who was a bully threatening the nation of Israel. Bullies use their strength or power to hurt others with words or actions. Be a friend to those who are being bullied. And tell a trusted adult.

You can read about David and Goliath in 1 Samuel, chapter 17.

Have you ever met a bully? Ask a trusted adult to help you make a plan for keeping safe the next time you do and make notes here.

David said to Saul, "Let no one lose heart on account of this Philistine; your servant will go and fight him."

1 SAMUEL 17:32, NIV

Jesus, thank you for giving me the strength to face hard situations. In your name, amen.

Wild Wonder

Goliath bird-eating spiderlings are about 0.75 inches (2 centimeters) in size—larger than some adult spiders of other species.

Creature Connection

In the story of David and Goliath, David chose 5 smooth stones from a stream. Collect a few stones. Then wash and dry them. Use paint or a permanent marker to write words or phrases on the stones to remind you to help others. You might find your own words and verses or use these: courageous (Joshua 1:9), trustworthy (Psalm 111:7), faithful (Matthew 25:21), honest (John 8:32), strong (Philippians 4:13).

Black Widow Spider

Scientific Names: *Latrodectus hasselti*, *Latrodectus mactans*, *Latrodectus hesperus*, and more

A Healthy Fear

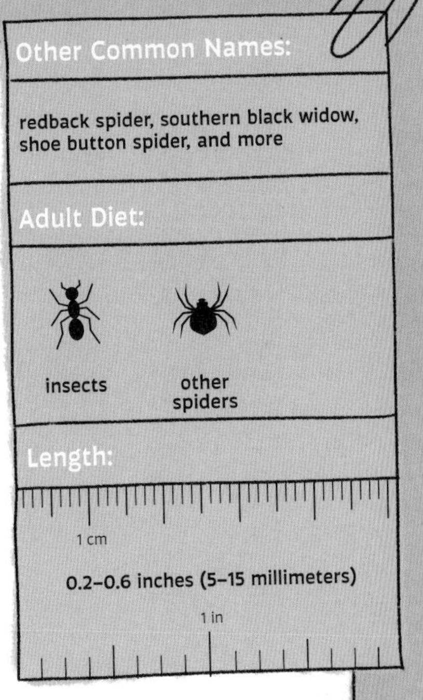

Other Common Names:
redback spider, southern black widow, shoe button spider, and more
Adult Diet:
insects
other spiders
Length:
1 cm
0.2–0.6 inches (5–15 millimeters)
1 in

When a woman's husband dies, she is called a widow. A person may wear black clothing to show they are mourning the death of a loved one. Black widow spiders were given their name because of the glossy black exoskeleton of females and because females have been known to eat their mates. But not all black widows are cannibals.

Though notorious, black widow spiders are rather shy. They even play dead when they feel threatened. Females can be found hanging upside down in their tangled webs, but the brown males are often hard to find because of their small size.

Birds and other spiders hunt for black widows. Bright-red spots, triangles, or hourglass shapes on the abdomen of a black widow warn most predators to stay away.

Like almost all spiders, black widows are venomous. They use their venom to kill their prey. Although 99.9 percent of all spider bites are not life-threatening to people, the bite of black widows is an exception. Black widow venom can cause serious complications and sometimes, though rarely, death. Medical treatment should begin right away.

Many people live in fear of spiders. Most spiders will not hurt us, but we still need to respect them. God is omnipotent, which means he's all-powerful. We don't need to be afraid of God, but we should know that his power and love are limitless. When the Bible says to "fear God," it means we should have a deep understanding and respect for him. This leads to trust and obedience. Talk to God today about how you honestly feel about him. He's listening.

With an adult's help, look up some more verses about fearing God. Choose a favorite one to record here.

The fear of the LORD is the beginning of wisdom, and knowledge of the Holy One is understanding.

PROVERBS 9:10, NIV

Heavenly Father, help me to live with appropriate fear (respect) for you. In Jesus' name, amen.

Wild Wonder

While a male black widow is looking for a mate, he does not eat.

Creature Connection

The Bible tells us to care for widows and orphans (see James 1:27). We should also care for single parents (and their children) as well as children who do not regularly see their parents. Talk to a grown-up about how you can help. Maybe you can do yard work, provide a meal, give school supplies, or be a friend.

Kipling's Jumping Spider

Scientific Name: *Bagheera kiplingi*

Surprising Diet

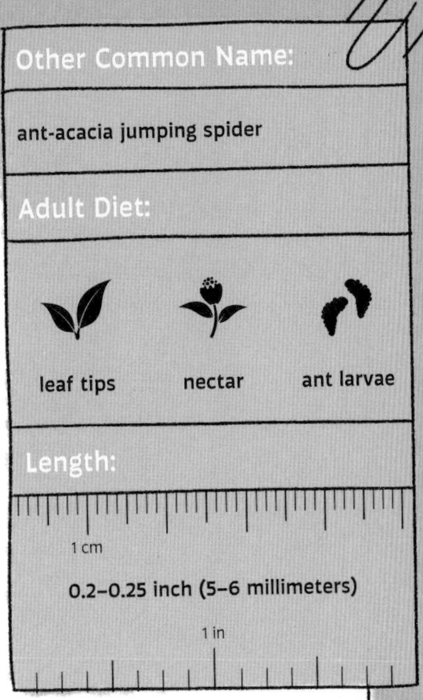

Other Common Name:
ant-acacia jumping spider
Adult Diet:
leaf tips
nectar
ant larvae
Length:
1 cm
0.2–0.25 inch (5–6 millimeters)
1 in

In Mexico and Central America, one spider stands out from all the other spiders. Kipling's jumping spider is not a fierce predator.

Even though Kipling's jumping spider has the same venom and fangs as other spiders, it's the only spider that intentionally and primarily eats plants. It's an herbivore. More than 90 percent of this spider's diet comes from acacia trees.

The leaves of the acacia tree have tiny, orange, sausage-shaped tips full of protein, sugar, and fiber. Kipling's jumping spiders eat these tips, which are called Beltian bodies. This spider lives only on the acacia tree. But it's not the only critter to live there.

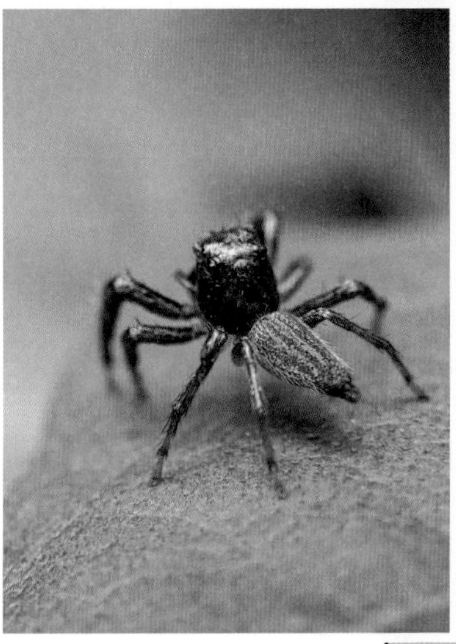

Ants also live on acacia trees. They protect and defend the tree from leaf-hungry critters who would otherwise kill the acacia tree—including the Kipling's jumping spider.

These spiders use their excellent eyesight along with smart strategies to avoid the ants. Kipling's jumping spiders build their nests at the tips of old leaves where the ants don't patrol.

Kipling's jumping spider was first discovered in the 1800s. But it wasn't until this century that scientists accidentally discovered that the spiders eat a vegetarian diet. Until then, it was assumed all spiders were predators. Sometimes we make assumptions about people based on what we think we know about them. It's easy to judge others based on what they show us, but there's always more to their stories. Thankfully, God sees your heart and the hearts of everyone else. God tells us not to judge others. Just love people with kindness, even if they make choices you don't agree with.

Have you been tempted to judge someone? Write some judgmental thoughts on the left side below. Then draw an arrow from each one and write a kind and loving thought on the right side.

Be kind and compassionate to one another, forgiving each other, just as in Christ God forgave you.

EPHESIANS 4:32, NIV

Lord, thank you for helping me to be kind and loving instead of judgmental. In Jesus' name, amen.

Wild Wonder

Kipling's jumping spiders (*Bagheera kiplingi*) are named after author Rudyard Kipling and his black panther character, Bagheera, in *The Jungle Book*.

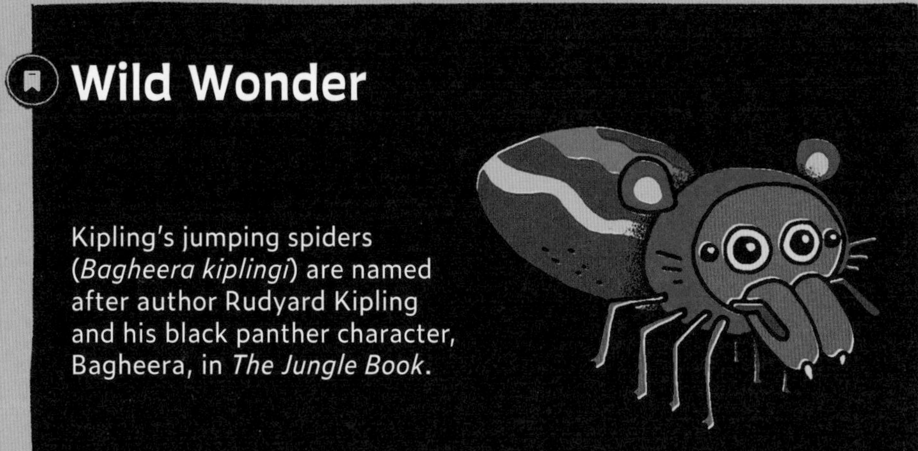

Creature Connection

If you typically eat meat as your main source of protein, create a menu for a full day (or meal) that includes no meat but is still high in protein. You might include beans, nuts, lentils, or eggs in your diet. Talk to an adult about your options and then enjoy your high-protein vegetarian food.

A Note to the Reader

Dear Reader,

This world God created amazes me. I had a lot of fun researching and writing the words you read in this book. The hardest part was deciding which animals to include and limiting them to only 52 wild wonders.

After reading *Quirky Critter Devotions*, I hope you are inspired by these incredible animals—and this entire world. Keep an eye out for more wild wonders and think about what each wonder can teach you or remind you about God.

I'd like to encourage you to keep learning about this world by getting outside. Photographs and facts in books help us to understand animals, but we can also connect with them in real life. Splash in a stream, hike in a forest, or turn over rocks in your backyard to engage with more creatures. Museums, aquariums, and zoos help us get up close and personal with animals we wouldn't typically meet in nature. Videos and live cams show us animals we might not be able to meet otherwise.

One of my favorite things about writing *Quirky Critter Devotions* is the chance to share how science and faith connect. As much as I celebrate your curiosity about animals, it's even more important to know Jesus in a personal way. This devotional is just the start. Read the words of God in the Bible and talk to him every day through prayer.

This world is full of quirky critters and wild wonders. If you see an interesting creature (whether it's listed in this book or not), take a picture or document it in a nature journal. I'd love to hear about it. You might have your grown-up tag me on social media or use #QuirkyCritterDevotions.

Live in wonder,

Annette Whipple

Learn More

You might access some of these websites in your research to learn more about animals. Ask a trusted adult if you read anything that confuses you or seems different from what you believe about God.

- audubon.org
- akronzoo.org/frogwatch
- birdsoftheworld.org
- dkfindout.com/uk/animals-and-nature
- easyscienceforkids.com
- explore.org/livecams
- journeynorth.org
- kids.nationalgeographic.com
- massaudubon.org/get-involved/community-science
- musicofnature.com/videos
- spiderid.com

The author has a book series for animal lovers. Ask for these and other books by the author at your local bookstore or library.

- *Whooo Knew? The Truth About Owls*
- *Woof! The Truth About Dogs*
- *Scurry! The Truth About Spiders*
- *Ribbit! The Truth About Frogs*
- *Meow! The Truth About Cats*
- *Chomp! The Truth About Sharks*

Acknowledgments

I wrote the words, but it took a whole team of people to create *Quirky Critter Devotions: 52 Wild Wonders for Kids*.

Wanting to create a fact-filled and hands-on devotional for children, I used Michelle Medlock Adams's book *Dinosaur Devotions* as my mentor text. As I crafted the book, my critique partners helped me write clearly and concisely. Animal experts answered my questions and encouraged me to celebrate my own curiosity during my years researching animals. My agent, Stacey Kondla with The Rights Factory, celebrated this book idea from the time she first learned of it. Thank you.

The Tyndale team has been so supportive of this project. I'm so grateful to Linda Howard for believing in *Quirky Critter Devotions*. Discussing book details and getting to know one another while hiking among redwoods will always be a fond memory. Debbie King made this a much better book by suggesting tweaks and adjustments as well as helping incorporate the journaling section of each devotion. Talia Messina has helped me to see the big picture and small details of this book's production. Sarah Susan Richardson made this book stand out with its beautiful design. The photography and illustrations invite readers to live in wonder of God's creation. I'm grateful for the entire Tyndale team who have worked hard to make this a book readers will connect with. Thank you.

Readers, you are also part of the book team. Without you, there wouldn't be a reason to write. Thank you.

I'm always grateful for my family's support, which makes my writing a possibility. Thank you.

And of course, God gets all the credit for creating amazing and unique quirky critters and inspiring me to look for faith connections. Thank you.

About the Author

Annette Whipple celebrates curiosity and inspires a sense of wonder while exciting readers about science and history. She's the author of many fact-filled children's books, including *The Laura Ingalls Wilder Companion: A Chapter-by-Chapter Guide* (Chicago Review Press), *The Story of the Wright Brothers* (Rockridge Press), and *Whooo Knew? The Truth About Owls* (Reycraft Books) in the Truth About series. While researching, Annette held a huge Eurasian eagle owl and a Brazilian whiteknee tarantula and met more wild wonders. When Annette's not reading or writing, you might find her baking for her family in Pennsylvania. Get to know Annette and explore her resources and learning guides at AnnetteWhipple.com and WilderCompanion.com.

Notes

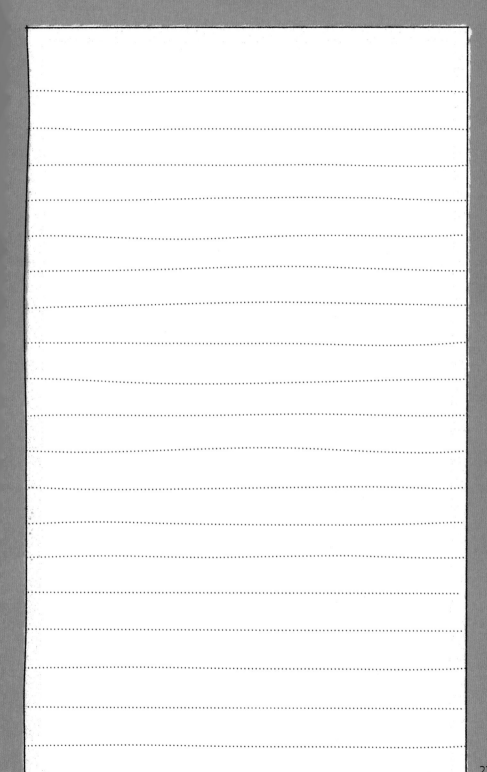